TWAYNE'S WORLD LEADERS SERIES

EDITORS OF THIS VOLUME

Arthur W. Brown
*Baruch College, The City University
of New York*

and

Thomas S. Knight
Adelphi University

Karl Marx

TWLS 70

Karl Marx

KARL MARX

By RICHARD E. OLSEN

Adelphi University

TWAYNE PUBLISHERS

A DIVISION OF G. K. HALL & CO., BOSTON

Library of Congress Cataloging in Publication Data

Olsen, Richard E   1941–
  Karl Marx.

  (Twayne's world leaders series; TWLS 70)
  Bibliography: pp. 189–91
  Includes index.
  1. Marx, Karl, 1818–1883.
HX39.5.O56   335.4′092′4 [B]   77–8164
ISBN 0–8057–7678–8

Contents

About the Author

Richard Olsen is an associate professor of philosophy at Adelphi University where he has taught since 1971. He received a B.S. in mathematics from Union College, Schenectady, New York in 1962 and his Ph.D. in philosophy from Brown University in 1971. His philosophical interests cover a wide area, with publications and addresses in the philosophy of science and the social sciences, the philosophy of logic and mathematics and Indian metaphysics. He has been active in both the socialist and the anti-Vietnam War movements. He has also for a time lived as a Theravadian Buddhist monk in Thailand, while studying Buddhist philosophy and meditation.

Preface

A book on Marx can hardly be entirely neutral in its viewpoint; but it can approach its subject with honesty. This book reflects a sympathetic reading of Marx; for his work is, I believe, in many ways even more relevant to the contemporary world than it was to the capitalism of his own century. I have strived in it, nonetheless, to be as objective as I possibly could be, and have nowhere simplified or quoted selectively in order to present this case. Consequently, it is a useful work for anyone who wants to understand what Marx was doing, considered carefully and from a broad perspective which avoids falling prey to the usual temptation to try to understand him too quickly or make him fit a preconceived ideological mold.

The book consists of seven chapters. It is designed in such a way that the reader should understand Marx's theories in greater and greater depth as he proceeds. At the same time, each new chapter covers a different and, within limits, isolatable general aspect of Marx's work. This dual character of the book is achieved by working with the most easily accessible aspects first in order to give the reader an overview which can provide the basis for an understanding of the relatively more complex ones to follow. Marx's theory fortunately lends itself easily to such an approach. Thus, after the opening biographical chapter, I present, in the next two chapters, Marx's theory of historical development without making explicit reference to either its dialectical structure or the general socioeconomic theory which he finds the basis of its capitalist phase. Having done this, that is, having given the reader some acquaintance with the theory's substance, I then pass on to the more formal questions of theoretical structure and method in the fourth chapter. This in its turn allows the final chapters on the development of Marx's full theory of capitalist society to be read with greater under-standing. The above dual character of the chapters also enables them to be used separately by someone who already has some familiarity with the subject; frequent references to prior chapters further facilitates such use.

Many people were helpful to me in preparing this book. I would like to thank in particular Marlene Fried, Joan Smith, Alan Schiffman, and Richard Schmitt, who read and commented upon early drafts of portions of the manuscript, and all of the members of the Marxist Activist Philosophers Association, whose helpful criticism of my ideas was invaluable to me in this work. My special thanks also go to Marvin Mandell, who nearly twenty years ago introduced me to the work of Marx, to Milton Fisk, who has taught me most about it, and to Prem Montano and the Zero Work Collective whose thoughts on contemprary revolutionary theory have done so much to stimulate my own. Finally, I want to thank the excellent typists who worked on the manuscript, Janet Olsen and Dorothy Schielein, together with Tina Kazemi who patiently helped me in its proof.

RICHARD OLSEN

Adelphi University

Chronology

1818 Karl Marx born May 5 in Trier in the Rhineland.

1835– Studies first at Bonn and then Berlin University; receives
1841 his doctorate *in absentia* from Jena University, April, 1841.

1842 Edits the liberal paper, *Rheinische Zeitung;* becomes interested in communist thought.

1843 Marries Jenny von Westphalen, June 19; moves with her to Paris in October to become coeditor with Arnold Ruge of the *Deutsch-Französische Jahrbücher.*

1844 Breaks with Ruge; works on the *Economic and Philosophical Manuscripts;* begins his partnership with Engels.

1847 Publishes *The Poverty of Philosophy,* a critique of the thought of Proudhon.

1848 Completes the manuscript of the *Communist Manifesto* for the Communist League; edits the *Neue Rheinische Zeitung* in Cologne during the German Revolution.

1849 Moves to London after the failure of the European revolutions of 1848; resumes his studies of capitalist society.

1859 Publishes *A Contribution to the Critique of Political Economy.*

1861 Begins work on *Capital.*

1864 Takes part in the founding of the International Working Men's Association; elected to its Provisional Committee, he drafts its Provisional Rules and Inaugural Address.

1867 Publishes the first volume of *Capital.*

1871 Defends the Paris Commune, becoming notorious in the process.

1872 Struggles with Bakunin for control of the International; this results in a split in the organization which leads to its subsequent demise.

1881 December 2, death of his wife, Jenny; Marx himself is in very poor health at the time.

1883 March 14, dies, in London at home.

CHAPTER 1

Theory and Practice:
Marx's Life and Work

HOW one reads Marx's character is largely a political matter. In reality, like anyone, his life and personality were as marked by contradiction as the society divided in struggle which he sought to describe. One is tempted thus to pick and choose traits according to what one wishes to make the man. If a fair list were given, however, it would seem reasonable to say that he was bad tempered, caustic, fierce, vain, self-sacrificing, selfish, whining, capable of great love, a good father, a lover of mankind, fatherly to all, honest, scrupulous, tender, brilliant, eminently rational, racist in an offhand manner, anti-Semitic, cynical, a man of vision, a person who developed irony as an art, a person who was obsessed with irony, obsessive in general, flexible, a brilliant politican, a sly politician, at times even an unscrupulous politician, but a candid one as they go. He was not timid, falsely modest, narrow, or slovenly; nor was he, as some among his critics claim, an unsubtle polemicist, an amateurish investigator prone to simple errors, a metaphysician on one level and a minor Ricardian economist on another, a metaphysician on any level, a Ricardian economist in any sense, an economist—in the sense that this term is used by economists— or a man who dreamed of himself as a future dictator of mankind or any portion thereof.

Marx was born in Trier, in the Rhineland, on May 5, 1818. His family was Jewish in origin on both sides, but his father, Hirshel, was nonreligious, a freethinker who admired the philosophers of the French Enlightenment. For convenience, in order to keep his law practice intact under the rigid administration of the Rhineland by Prussia which followed the end of the Napoleonic Wars, he had the family baptized in the

11

Lutheran church when Karl was six. He himself changed his name to the Christian "Heinrich" upon baptism; Jewish cultural influence, already minimal, seems from this point onward to be nonexistent in the life of young Marx; he does not, at least, ever identify himself with the Jews and appears to have had a somewhat contemptuous attitude toward them all his life.

In 1835, at the age of seventeen, he matriculated at Bonn University. His plans at this time seem to involve following in his father's footsteps as a lawyer—at least in the long range; for he was far from studious his first year in the university and appears to have spent more time in beer halls than classrooms. After he had managed to get himself arrested for public intoxication and received his mandatory dueling scar, Heinrich Marx decided to enroll him in the Berlin University, an establishment far more noted for its sobriety than Bonn. The atmosphere seems to have effected Karl. For the next four years at Berlin he proved himself a brilliant student. Although entering the university in the faculty of law, he also attended lectures in philosophy. The subject in time became a passion for him, gradually replacing, to a large extent, an earlier passion for literature. Hegel's works at the time still dominated the German academic scene and Marx became—while still an undergraduate— a respected interpreter of Hegel. He was treated as a peer by the older, more established philosophers Moses Hess and Bruno Bauer, and enjoyed a reputation for brillance in the circle they frequented, the Young Hegelians, a group which opposed the official theological and politically conservative interpretation of Hegel with their own ultrarationalist, freethinking, enlightenment-oriented version.[1]

From relatively early Marx seems to have been interested in the political implications of the Hegelian philosophy—in general to a greater extent than most of his Young Hegelian allies. But even the least political expressions of discontent or dissent proved too much for the Prussian authorities. Hoping to gain an appointment at Bonn through the influence of his friend Bauer, who had recently received a lectureship there, and finding it increasingly difficult to express unorthodox ideas on any subject at Berlin, Marx sent his doctoral thesis to the University of Jena, where dissertations were accepted *in absentia.*

He received his doctorate from Jena on April 15, 1841, only to find the following October that Bauer had lost his position at Bonn because of his open avowal of atheism.

The dissertation which Marx sent to Jena was entitled "On the Difference Between the Philosophies of Nature of Democritus and Epicurus," indicating an interest already at this date in materialist viewpoints. This interest was strengthened soon after by the publication in the same year of Ludwig Feuerbach's *The Essence of Christianity,* a critique of religion which broke not only with theological spiritualism but also with the rationalized and rarefied spirituality of Hegel's philosophical idealism. Bauer had not made this latter break—never moving, as Feuerbach had done, to a fully naturalistic standpoint. He, moreover, was politically quietistic, believing that—as development of the human spirit was the main task which confronted humanity —critical thought, the propagation of a militant atheism, and not social action, was the only means of transforming the world. Marx, for these reasons, soon drew away from him. Failing to get his university appointment, he turned to journalism, becoming, on the recommendation of Moses Hess, editor in chief of the liberal Cologne newspaper, the *Rheinische Zeitung,* in the fall of 1842. With this change in orientation, his political interests blossomed. Not only did he break with Bauer; he also severed relations with the Young Hegelians generally, refusing to publish their attacks on religion in the paper, which had hitherto been their domain. This suited both the Prussian censors and the Rhenish businessmen who financed the paper quite well; the liberal democracy which he advocated also sat well with the latter, though with the former it eventually put him at odds. In March, 1843, in order to avoid the closing of the *Rheinische Zeitung* by the censors, Marx was forced to resign as editor.[2] On April 1, the censors closed the paper anyway.

The following June Marx married Jenny von Westphalen, a neighbor in Trier since his childhood and his fiancée since his university days. Jenny was socially his superior, coming from an aristocratic family, but the match was—even despite Marx's somewhat dubious prospects at this point—unopposed. Jenny's father, an Enlightenment liberal like his own, had been Marx's mentor during his adolescence and both loved and admired the young man. He was, by the time of the marriage, already dead, but apparently his opinion still held sway in the family. The couple, moreover, were known to be deeply in love.

During the spring and summer of 1843, Marx, now unemployed, wrote several essays. His "Critique of Hegel's Doctrine of the State," his "On the Jewish Question," and much of "A Contribution to the Critique of Hegel's Philosophy of Right" date from this period. The first, although still heavily influenced by Feuerbach, lays the groundwork, as we will see, for his own method after his move to communism; it also anticipates much in his later views on the social function of the state. The second, on the Jewish question, does so as well, incorporating also an attack on contemporary "civil society," that is, capitalist social relations, as a part of his critique of the bifurcation of society into this civil society and the false communalism of the state. The last article is still more explicitly communist and revolutionary; in it, for the first time, Marx identifies the working class as the instrument of social change. The first article was never published during Marx's lifetime; the latter two, however, were. They appeared at the beginning of the following year, 1844, in the *Deutsch-Französische Jahrbücher*, a journal which Marx coedited with Arnold Ruge in Paris, having moved there convinced that he could not, given his politics, pursue a career in journalism within Germany. Ruge, who had, like Marx, been affiliated with the Young Hegelians and who, also like him, was far more political than most, remained his colleague nonetheless only a short time. Marx and he, whose politics up until this point had been extremely similar, parted company within five months as their political differences became more problematic. Ruge was still a liberal in early 1844, while Marx was becoming a communist revolutionary.

Marx's interest in communism—a doctrine then fashionable in radical intellectual circles—had begun in a rather strange way. At the time when he had become the editor of the *Rheinische Zeitung*, the paper was under attack as communist due to the publication in it of an article by Moses Hess, who had recently adopted the position. Marx, in fact, was brought in as editor of the paper by Hess in part to calm this and other disputes which were making the paper's bourgeois benefactors anxious. He at the time knew very little about communism and set out to study it in order to engage more knowledgeably in the controversy. The study gradually, over the period of about a year, led him to accept the doctrine, though he always maintained some critical distance between himself and the communist writers he had read. An exception to this tendency of critical acceptance is found in his reaction to an article published in the *Jahrbücher,* entitled "Outlines of a Critique of Political Economy," for which he had unbounded enthusiasm. On reading it he immediately began his own study of the political economists, which led soon after to his first detailed study of the struggle between capital and labor, the work which is generally known as the *Economic and Philosophical Manuscripts of 1844.*[3] The author of the article which had so energized Marx was Frederick Engels. They had met once in 1842 at the *Rheinische Zeitung* offices, but Marx, being busy and thinking Engels just another Young Hegelian from Berlin, had been formal and cold with him at the time; and they had not had any real exchange of ideas. When they met for a second time in August, 1844, in Paris, however, they began a collaboration which would last for the rest of their lives.

Engels was also Rhenish, from the industrial town of Barmen, but his family background was quite different from that of either Marx *or* Marx's wife. Engels was an actual bourgeois, his family owning textile mills in both Barmen and Manchester, England. At the time of their first 1842 meeting in fact, he was en route to Manchester where he was to learn the family business. He also planned, though not with his family's consent, to study the Chartist movement of the English workers and the situation of the workers generally in England while there.[4] He had that same year been converted to communism by Moses Hess. Like Marx, he had moved to it via contact with the Young Hegelians followed by an interest in Feuerbach; but with this difference; his initial moves to radical views on politics and religion had met strong opposition from his father who was, unlike Marx's liberal and freethinking one, a tyrannical and

stodgy Pietist Protestant, while his final move set him at complete odds with both family and class. Engels was a member
of that section of the bourgeoisie which, as Marx and he were
to write later in the *Manifesto*, "cuts itself adrift and joins . . .
the class that holds the future in its hands."[5]

In September, 1844, the two young men began to attend
meetings of French workers' groups together. Communism at
this time had already made some inroads into the working class
as well as the intelligensia. The movement, in fact, had its
origins in both. While post-Enlightenment intellectuals began
to speculate on the structure and possibility of Utopian communal societies, some of which, like Claude-Henri Saint-Simon's,
still retained current class relations (though miraculously grown
benevolent), a home-grown, more egalitarian variety of communist speculations and organizations emerged, mainly among craft
workers, in all parts of Western Europe.[6] These societies were
a legacy of the left wing of the Jacobin movement of the French
Revolution, for whom that revolution with its ideology of "liberty,
equality, and fraternity" had been decidedly left unfinished.
A second attempt at revolution in 1830, having likewise failed
to establish these ideals, had at least revived them and suc-
cessors to the original left-Jacobin organizations. Styling themselves on "Gracchus" Babeuf's secret organization in the 1789
Revolution, they tended to be conspiratorial, despite their egali-
tarianism, and were often crankish in their approach; but they
did represent the beginnings of socialist workers' organizations
in continental Europe.[7]

At any rate, they were apparently thought dangerous enough
that foreign communists in France were liable to expulsion on
short notice. Thus, on January 11, 1845, Marx and two other
foreign radicals—one of them the Russian revolutionist, Bakunin
—were given notice to leave France. To return to Germany was
out of the question; since the previous April there had been a
warrant out in Prussia for both Marx's and Ruge's arrest for
treason because of their activities in connection with the
Jahrbücher. Marx received permission to live in Belgium so long
as he stayed out of Belgian politics, and moved to Brussels with
his wife, their housekeeper, and a nine month old daughter
on February third. In Brussels he continued the theoretical work

which he and Engels had already begun together in Paris. *The Holy Family,* their attack on Bruno Bauer's philosophy, was already complete; it was published on February 24. That spring he made the famous notes for his never-to-be-written essay on Feuerbach which Engels published after his death as "Theses on Feuerbach." In the fall they began *The German Ideology* together. The summer had been occupied with a trip with Engels to England to study the workers' movement there.

The Chartists, who took their name from the People's Charter which they had presented to Parliament, urging universal male suffrage and other extensions of democracy in Britian, were at that time still providing the leadership for the English labor movement; and Marx attended a Chartist conference in London while there. The industrial revolution had begun earliest and developed furthest in Britain; politically the country was already firmly in the hands of its bourgeoisie and enjoyed a reasonable degree of democracy. Consequently, at this point in its development, the British workers' movement was organized relatively openly and was advanced enough to be pressing for political changes through mass organizations—although these organizations were still for the most part limited to the most skilled workers. Although revolutionists, Marx and Engels considered such approaches far superior to the conspiratorial approach prevalent on the Continent and a necessary step in the workers' self-organization to prepare themselves for revolution, a process which obviously must involve not only the mere seizure of power, but also the ability to keep it and use it for the transformation of society to communism once power is seized. The Chartists' demands, they felt, must necessarily lead them closer to this revolutionary transformation of society, and they desired to further politicize the European movement, hopefully, eventually in a setting of bourgeois democracy, so that mass political action would be possible also there.

To this end, they attempted both to influence the movement in Europe and to give it a greater cohesion. During the next year, 1846, they formed a Communist Correspondence Committee in Brussels, made efforts to convene an all-communist congress, and joined a small but multinational communist organization called The League of the Just. The League was a secret conspiratorial group when Marx and Engels joined it, but, under their influence, became instead a society for propagating communist theory, changing its name in the summer of 1847 to the Communist League. In a congress of the League, in the late fall of that year, Marx was commissioned to write the *Manifesto of the Communist Party* for it, an essay which has become his most famous—though it is not, unfortunately, his most accurate—work.[8] The essay, which gives a somewhat distorted summary of his and Engels's theory, together with a program for a workers' government, is based on a draft which Engels had written before the congress met. The final version was completed by Marx at the end of January, 1848, after the Central Committee of the League, grown tired of waiting, had given him a February 1 deadline for it.

It was published in a German edition in London later that month, at about the time when the first of the many revolutions of 1848 broke out in Paris. In early March, Marx received an invitation from a member of the French Provisional Government to return to revolutionary Paris; two days later he was expelled from Belgium. This time it was with three children that he and his wife, Jenny, moved; Jenny, the eldest daughter, now aged three years, a second daughter, Laura, of about two and a half and a baby, Edgar, whom they called "Musch," who had been born less than three months before. Events surrounding the expulsion were extremely unpleasant; Marx had given most of his recently acquired inheritance from his father to a fund to arm the Belgian workers who had joined the general agitation that was then beginning in Brussels; he was, consequently, arrested before his deportation; Jenny in her search of the police stations to find him, was also arrested. Both were released, however, on the following morning, and sent on their way to France.

Marx remained in Paris for only a month. The revolution in Germany was now well underway, and he and Engels returned to the Rhineland in order to engage in revolutionary journalism and organizing in their native land. Circles formerly associated with the *Rheinische Zeitung* in Cologne were again setting up a democratic daily; the two men managed to obtain control of it and began publication under the title *Neue Rheinische Zeitung* at the beginning of June. The paper was subtitled "An Organ of Democracy" and, in fact, for the most part, limited its propagandizing to the need for a democratic and unified Germany through the greater part of its existence; it was not, that is to say, an explicitly communist or even an exclusively working-class publication—though, in disputes within the democratic camp, it did always take the workers' part in an uncompromising fashion. Marx and Engels's reasoning in engaging on such a course was again based on the necessity of further politicizing the European workers' movement and allowing it to develop within the optimum conditions of a democratic government. There was a strong Workingmen's Union in Cologne, but it hardly amounted to a Communist Party; nor could it become one, they reasoned, since its leader, Dr. Andreas Gottschalk, failed to see the need for all democratic forces to work in unison to overcome the feudal stranglehold on Germany before the working class could strike off on its own; from Marx and Engels's viewpoint, Gottschalk's desire for class purity in actions was premature; German labor was in no position to fight its own battles before the bourgeois revolution had even been won. What *could* be done under the circumstances, however, was the further political organization of labor within a democratic front.

Such a policy drew attacks from Gottschalk and his supporters who accused Marx and Engels of insincerity in their love for the oppressed; they had, according to Gottschalk, merely a scientific and doctrinaire interest in the workers. The debate split the Workingmen's Union. It was silenced soon, however, as the forces of reaction took the offensive, transforming the living issues into theoretical ones once more. By late 1848, Marx had given up his hopes for the German bourgeoisie's revolutionary abilities and turned his attention more to working-class organizing; he was also now under indictment for incitement to rebellion. A friendly Rhenish jury acquitted him in February, 1849, after he had explained to them—in a speech which earned him a compliment from the jury's foreman—that his "crime" was in fact no crime at all since the matters at hand were political and not legal. A few months later, however, the Prussian government expelled him from the country. He had, in an effort to avoid further Prussian persecution, rather rashly given up his citizenship in late 1845, and now they took advantage of this move.

Marx returned to Paris in the beginning of June after publishing an explicitly communist final issue of the *Neue Rheinische Zeitung* in red newsprint. In July the French government told him that he could only stay in France on the condition he accept exile in Brittany. Declining this unattractive offer, he decided to move to London. He left Paris in late August to find lodging there for his family. Jenny, now pregnant with a fourth child, joined him a few weeks later. The child, Heinrich Guido, called "Föxchen," born two months after her arrival, was to live for less than a year.

The major leaders of the old Communist League one by one, in the wake of the reaction, found themselves refugees in England that year. Marx reorganized the League toward the end of summer and Engels joined him and the others late in the fall. He had had an adventurous time in the last days of the German Revolution, practicing soldiering as he had done formerly in his days with the Prussian cavalry, engaging in several actions in the Palantine campaign. The two now planned together a journal, *The Neue Rheinische Zeitung Politisch-Ökonomische Revue,* six issues of which came out during 1850, carrying in serial form Marx's work, *The Class Struggles in France, 1848–1850.* The journal, however, was far from a means of making a living. Engels, who was running out of money, was forced to reenter the family business in Manchester in order to support himself and help the Marxes get by; Marx, a short time after, obtained work as a European correspondent for the *New York Daily Tribune,* which took some of the financial burden from Engels, but added a different one in its stead. For Marx knew little English yet, so that Engels had to write most of the initial articles for him; also, there was the matter of his studies, for which Engels, understanding his friend's genius, was willing to sacrifice his own time. Although Marx, as he learned English, gradually took over responsibility for the *Tribune* articles, he continued to rely on Engels heavily for research; his own studies in political economy—by mutual consent—took precedence over the journalism to whatever extent it was possible for them to do so. He began to work at home and in the British Museum, reviving the research in politics and political economy that had ended with the publication of his attack on Proudhon's understanding of social and economic issues in *The Poverty of Philosophy* in 1847, when the call to activism of 1848 had intervened.

Despite Engels's assistance and the *Tribune* articles, this was a time of extreme poverty for the Marx family. Evicted from their first two lodgings in London, they finally had to settle in a squalid two-room flat in Soho; a move to a slightly larger three-room one on the same street later in the year proved only a minor improvement. Jenny gave birth to a daughter, Franziska, in the spring of 1851; when the child died a year later, the family had to borrow money to buy her a coffin. Furniture, family heirlooms, even articles of clothing—everything they had was subject to sale or a trip to the pawnshop at short notice. Whatever savings they had had long before disappeared into the accounts of the *Neue Rheinische Zeitung* during the revolution. Marx, despite the onset of a severe case of hemorrhoids—the first in a series of illnesses which would trouble him through the rest of his life—continued to work through all this; Jenny Marx—without even the work to sustain her, limited in her contacts in a strange country—managed to survive.

Yet even with the poverty of this period, the family appears to have been a warm and loving one. The cantankerousness for which Marx was famous in his political life did not extend to his intimate relations; his children loved him and he spent much time with them, playing and telling them stories; on the days when he worked at home on his most famous piece of political analysis, *The Eighteenth Brumaire of Louis Bonaparte*, during the winter of 1851–1852, the children are supposed to have played "horsey" on his back as he wrote.

Such conviviality does not, however, mark the history of his dealings with the Communist League in this period. In the beginning of 1850, Marx and Engels, along with their fellow exiles, believed the revolution could still be revived; but their study of current economic conditions, which indicated a developing boom, dissuaded them of this view later in the year.[9] Revolutionary action, they reasoned quite rightly, cannot be resparked under such conditions; to try to do so is both futile

and foolhardy. The workers' movement must develop slowly
at any rate, and gain experience and solidity before it can
conquer political power; there is no way to hurry it beyond a
point. Marx especially was always cautious about urging people
to insurrectionary action prematurely, exhibiting the patience of
a careful gardener for the movement he would spend his life
helping to grow. A faction in the League led by August Willich
and Karl Schapper from the Cologne Workingmen's Union
disagreed with Marx and Engels's analysis and advocated trying
to incite an uprising in Germany. The disagreement led to a
split. The League was further weakened by the arrest of many
of its members still within Germany. With the German section
in disarray and no real prospects for revolution in sight, it could
not exist for long. On November 17, 1852, the membership
of Marx and Engels's branch voted to disband.

The two men would not enter active politics again directly
for the next twelve years. During this time, however, Marx's
research in political economy blossomed and began to bear
fruit; the notebooks known as the "Grundrisse," which he wrote
during the winter of 1857–1858, allowed him to begin work
on *A Contribution to the Critique of Political Economy* the
following summer. The first part of it was published less than a
year later. He began work thereafter on a projected second part,
but scrapped the project and began over again in the late
spring of 1861. The new work, *Capital*, was to comprise four
volumes;[10] its approach, though highly theoretical, would presuppose no prior technical knowledge, so that an intelligent
working man could read it, a technique which at times—despite
its many aesthetic excellences—renders it unwieldly.[11] He began
to work on volumes one and four (known in English as "Theories
of Surplus Value") simultaneously, never completing the latter,
but publishing the former six years later in 1867.

The period after the disbanding of the Communist League
also brought some relief domestically to Marx, but much sorrow
as well. A daughter, Eleanor, whom they called "Tussy," was
born in January, 1855; later in the year, however, eight year
old "Musch" died, leaving Marx with the feeling that he knew
only now "for the first time what a real misfortune is."[12] Still
later in the year Jenny's mother also died, leaving her a fairly

small sum, but enough for the family to move from Soho. In October, 1856, they moved into a house in Maitland Park on Haverstock Hill, a London suburb. The family still was far from financially secure; and things were not helped by Marx's losing in 1860 a great deal of money on a pamphlet he published in connection with a feud he was having with Karl Vogt, the German liberal bourgeois exile leader whom he suspected—rightly, as it turned out—of being an agent of Napoleon III.

This affair, which clearly revealed the differences among the bourgeois and radical German exiles, was his closest approach to political activity during the period, apart from his articles in the *Tribune* and various leftist periodicals. He was in contact always with Ferdinand Lassalle, the German socialist leader of the time—especially after the prospects for revolution looked brighter following the economic crisis of 1857—but, as Marx could not himself operate in Germany, he could influence Lassalle and the German movement only indirectly through Wilhelm Liebknecht and his other followers there; his relations with Lassalle were, moreover, at best always ambivalent. Though greatly influenced by Marx's theory, Lassalle had his own ideas on political questions; he was also inclined toward opportunism, which made Marx suspicious of him; and he had nearly unlimited ambition, which provoked Marx's jealousy. On the one hand, Lassalle was for him the energetic leader which the movement in Germany needed; on the other, he was an upstart, who stole Marx's ideas, advancing his career by serving them out in a watered-down form.[13] The delicate relation between the two ended in August, 1864, when Lassalle was killed by a young Rumanian aristocrat in a duel over a woman.

One month later Marx entered active politics again on attending the meeting which founded the International Working Men's Association in London. This organization, which had grown out of contacts between English and French labor leaders made during a meeting in support of the Polish insurrection of 1863, reflected the new offensive undertaken by labor in the late 1850s and early 1860s in response to the above-mentioned business crisis of 1857. At a meeting called by the London Trades Council on the day after the meeting on Poland, to which this time only working-class representatives were invited, the problem of the use of foreign labor in strikebreaking was discussed and the need for international cooperation of labor as a solution was advanced. After a delay of over a year, a second meeting was convened and the International was founded. Marx, whose invitation to the meeting by Cremer of the Trades Council is still something of a mystery, managed, once he was there, to get himself elected to the Association's Provisional Committee; once on the Provisional Committee, he showed himself the only member capable of directing it successfully, and was given the charter to draft the Association's Provisional Rules and Inaugural Address. He managed to do so to the satisfaction of all, while basically writing his own political program into the documents—in rather mild language, it is true, but with only minor compromises in substance—an accomplishment that was no mean feat;[14] for very diverse elements had entered into association in the International; German communists, ex-Chartists, Polish émigrés, English followers of the Utopian Socialist Robert Owen, French adherents of Auguste Blanqui's conspiratorial tactics, initially, even some liberal Italian democrats. Finally, and most importantly, there were two main groups that needed satisfying, the militant but nonrevolutionary English trade unionists and the revolutionary but —with regard to strikes and other labor actions at least—nonmilitant French followers of Proudhon. The latter group also had tendencies toward anarchism, but, fortunately, was of late becoming more political; so that the Inaugural Address' call to the working class to "conquer political power" was not at the time overly offensive to them. The former group, the trade unionists, having always been political, could, also fortunately, read this phrase as well as the Provisional Rules' call for the "abolition of all class rule" in terms of their ongoing movement for manhood suffrage; the Address' reference to the eventual disappearance of hired wage labor, though weightier, apparently was too distant-sounding for them to take offense.

With Marx as the guiding spirit of its General Council, the International grew in power and prestige during the late 1860s. Internal strife—largely between Marx and the trade unionists on the one hand and the Proudhonists on the other—was always present; but the organization was still viable and healthy. Marx's personal influence on its politics also increased in certain quarters, as he won over a section of the Proudhonists; the English trade unionists, however, although on concrete issues he could usually count them as allies, he never was able to move farther to the left. Their leaders, in fact, increasingly used the growing organization, not as a political vehicle in itself, but only to keep international contacts; in 1868, some among them even sold out to the British Liberal Party, receiving bribes for rallying labor to its side.

This was not Marx's only disappointment in the International. The followers of Lassalle having rejected affiliation with the organization, it never had much influence in Germany; and its membership and affiliates never really represented the full spectrum of labor, being limited largely to skilled workers, as were most of the organizations of the time. Still, both Marx and Engels, who, though playing a less active part, was constantly in consultation with Marx concerning the International's policies, saw it as an important vehicle for further organization and as an invaluable tool during periods of insurrection. Their hopes for it were to fade, however, by the early 1870s. Two factors led to the International's decline and eventual dissolution: the first was the uprising of the Paris Commune; the second, the struggle for power within the organization between Bakunin and Marx.

The Paris Commune, founded March 18, 1871, followed events in the wake of the Franco-Prussian War. The French dictator, Louis Napoleon, having been defeated by the Prussians in a matter of weeks, France was declared a Republic on September 4, 1870. The Prussians, who had originally claimed only to be defending themselves against Bonaparte's aggression. nonetheless continued the war with France, signing an armistice only in late January, 1871.[15] A short time after, the new French Republic decided to disarm the National Guard which it had formed as a part of its war efforts; consisting of volunteers, largely recruited from the working class and lower-middle-class tradesmen, it was thought to be too dangerous a force to keep intact in time of peace. The attempted disarmament was extremely ill timed, coinciding with the week when a moratorium on debts, declared earlier by the Republic, fell due.[16] This seems to have forged an instant alliance between the workers and the tradesmen or petit bourgeoisie, as well as those peripheral elements of the bourgeoisie who were heavily in debt. Paris and a few other cities resisted the Republic's attempt and the Commune was declared.[17] The Republic, now headquartered in Versailles, responded immediately, putting down the insurrection—with the cooperation of the Prussians—by the end of May. Reprisals were severe; thousands were executed or deported to penal colonies; photographs of the time show fashionable ladies witnessing the executions, as if on a holiday; feelings ran high and the bourgeoisie was bent on instilling fear in the lower classes, having a need to prove its power to itself, in the face of its own fears, as well.

From the beginning Marx had opposed an insurrection in the city, urging the workers to support the new Republic on its founding in a message from the International's General Council which condemned Prussia's continuation of the war. An insurrection would, he felt, be doomed to failure; the best course for the working class would be to continue its organization under the Republic; after twenty stultifying years of Louis Bonaparte's dictatorship, it had little cohesion and was hardly in a position to govern; the Republic offered it a chance to develop for a successful seizure of power at a future time. When the workers failed to take his advice, and instead formed their alliance with the middle and petit bourgeoisie, he nevertheless gave them full support in their undertaking, rallying the General Council behind them and ultimately issuing an address in praise of the Commune in the International's name.[18] This led to many hysterical accusations against the International as a conspiratorial organization and turned the—until then—relatively obscure Marx into the notorious "Red Doctor" overnight. The pressure was too great for many of the English trade unionists; several left the organization, weakening it considerably. What was left of the French section, moreover, was a disruptive and bitter group of exiles; French labor itself—as well as labor on the Continent generally—was greatly hampered in its development for several years.

Simultaneous with these developments, the battle between Marx and the General Council and the anarchist revolutionary Bakunin and his followers was tearing the International apart.

Bakunin, opposing both the emphasis on the political in the organization and the centralism of its General Council, never managed to carry a majority in the International; but on his expulsion from it in 1872, he retained enough power to cripple it with a split. The expulsion itself was a somewhat sordid affair in which fact and innuendo were mixed indiscriminately by both sides, Marx and Engels, apparently disingenuously, exaggerating Bakunin's contacts with the Russian terrorist, Sergei Nietchayev, in order to strengthen the more legitimate side of their case. Bakunin having been expelled, Engels—in order to keep the General Council out of Bakuninist hands—proposed moving it to New York, a motion which passed by a narrow majority. Four years later it disbanded at a conference in Philadelphia. The Bakuninist portion of the organization lasted another five years until 1881.

This sudden departure from active politics at least gave Marx more of an opportunity to continue his work on *Capital*. A life annuity of three hundred and fifty pounds per year from Engels, beginning in 1868, also was of help. Except for his contacts with the socialist party in Germany, which had managed a reconciliation of its Marxist and Lassallean sections in 1875, this work occupied most of his time after the International's split.[19] By 1880, though he had not yet completed the second volume, he was simultaneously at work on volume three. Unfortunately, also during this period, his health began to fail. After the death of his wife in December, 1882, he traveled on the Continent, visiting health spas and his married daughters there. When the eldest of them, her mother's namesake, Jenny, died less than a year after the mother, at the age of only thirty-eight, it was a hard second blow for Marx. He himself died only two months later, on March 14, 1883, at home in his study in the middle of the afternoon. He was sixty-four years of age.

Marx was survived by his two daughters, Laura and Eleanor. The second and third volumes of *Capital* were compiled and published by Engels from Marx's unfinished manuscripts in 1885 and 1894. Engels himself lived twelve years after Marx's death, dying the year after seeing the third volume through the press, on August 5, 1895.

CHAPTER 2

History as Struggle: Class and Otherwise

"THE history of all hitherto existing society," Marx tells us in the 1848 *Manifesto of the Communist Party*, "is the history of class struggles," struggles which "now hidden, now open fight . . . each time ended either in a revolutionary reconstitution of society at large or in the common ruin of the contending classes."[1] There follows a list of the antagonists—"free man and slave, patrician and plebeian, lord and serf, guild master and journeyman." These he then places under the broader headings "oppressor and oppressed," adding to the list the "two great classes directly facing each other" in modern times, the bourgeoisie or capitalist class and the proletariat, the class of wage workers. Whereas in earlier societies social gradations tended to be complex, in the current epoch they are, he says, in the process of being simplified, as classes formed in earlier times dissolve and the middle classes—shopkeepers, small tradesmen and peasants—sink into the proletariat; so that society increasingly divides into these "two great hostile camps," a capitalist elite on the one side and the mass of workers on the other.

The history of the coming into being of the modern epoch he then sketches somewhat hastily. Medieval towns, formed largely by serfs who had escaped from the countryside, were originally founded on skilled handicraft industry, its practitioners being organized into monopolistic "closed guilds." With the discovery of America and the rounding of the Cape of Good Hope, however, increased trade led to the obsolescence of the guild system which "now no longer sufficed for the growing wants of the new markets" in the American colonies and Asia.[2] A system of manufacturing whereby "the division of labor between the different corporate guilds vanished in the face of division of labor in each single workshop" replaced the old guild system while "the

28

manufacturing middle class" likewise replaced the guild masters. As the market continued to grow, the system of manufacturing was in its turn replaced by the "steam and machinery" of industrial production; the "industrial middle class" was replaced by "industrial millionaires, the leaders of whole industrial armies, the modern bourgeois." As the power of modern industry grew, establishing a world market for its goods, so also did that of the class that owned and controlled it. Coming into being through a "long course of development of a series of revolutions in the modes of production and exchange," the bourgeoisie finally succeeded in pushing "into the background every class handed down from the Middle Ages." In each stage of its development, there can be marked a corresponding stage in its "political advance."[3] When it reaches full maturity, "the executive of the modern state is but a committee for managing the common affairs of the whole bourgeoisie."

This class is by far the most dynamic that has ever appeared in human history. It "cannot exist without constantly revolutionising the instruments of production" thereby constantly disturbing existing social relations as well as constantly producing a greater mass of goods. With this ever-expanding production, moreover, the "need of a constantly expanding market for its products" arises, and the influence of the bourgeoisie is felt throughout the world. It subjects the countryside to the rule of the city and makes "barbarian and semi-barbarian countries dependent on the civilized ones." Hence it both centralizes politics nationally and internationally brings a "cosmopolitan character" to the national life of even the most backward and narrowly provincial regions on earth.

But the forces that it calls forth in its constant technological progress begin finally to undermine its own existence, while the bourgeoisie stands before them, says Marx, "like the sorcerer who is no longer able to control the powers of the nether world whom he has called up by his spells." Periodic commercial crises "put on trial, each time more threateningly, the existence of the entire bourgeois society." Overproduction—"an epidemic that in all earlier epochs would have seemed an absurdity"—is the culprit in such crises; the existence of "too much civilization, too much means of subsistence, too much industry, too much commerce" devastates society as surely as any war.[4] Consequently, a part of the already established productive forces are of necessity destroyed while, as the only other alternative, new markets for the excess production are eagerly sought, thereby "paving the way for more extensive and more destructive crises" in the future.

In all this the bourgeoisie has not only "forged the weapons that bring death to itself" but also "called into existence the men who are to wield those weapons"—namely, the proletarians. For this class of necessity develops simultaneously with the bourgeoisie. From its birth it is the latter's antagonist. Yet it at the same time is united by and with the bourgeoisie in its struggle with the former social order; ironically, it is the capitalists themselves, in pursuit of their political ends, who first bring coherence to the class. As time goes by, however, and the uncertainty of bourgeois conditions assail it while its numbers all the while continue to grow, it becomes a class for itself. Competition for work among class members themselves may continually upset its unity, but "it ever rises up again, stronger, firmer, mightier" as the struggle continues. The bourgeoisie, says Marx, has produced "its own gravediggers. Its fall and the victory of the proletariat are equally inevitable."[5] With this victory, moreover, will come—after a transitional period in which the proletariat "makes itself the ruling class"—an end to the conditions which make for a class structured society. Abolishing classes generally in the course of abolishing bourgeois social relations, the proletariat necessarily abolishes also itself, and hence "will thereby have abolished its own supremacy as a class." Society then will enter a qualitatively new phase of social development in which it becomes "an association in which the free development of each is the condition for the free development of all."

This summary of historical development in the *Manifesto* is, though at points enlightening and on the whole compatible with the rest of Marx's writings on history, nonetheless still a summary; as such it is subject to oversimplification, as well as omission. Its sketchy treatment of class and class struggle leave one somewhat unclear as to what a class even is for Marx, let alone what it means for history to consist of the struggle of these entities. The work's dual function as theoretical statement and political polemic compounds these problems even more. Having first taken this broad overview, we may see more clearly what both class and history are for Marx and how the two are related through the notion of class struggle, by turning to his account of the variety of socioeconomic forms found within the *entire* spectrum of historical and pre-historic society.

Sources for this account are relatively scattered and cover a fairly long time span in Marx's career, the majority occurring in *The German Ideology* (1845–1846), the chapter on capital in the "Grundrisse" notebooks (1857–1858) and *Capital,* both Volume I (published in 1867) and Volume III (published posthumously in 1894). They nonetheless comprise a reasonably coherent whole which develops, both in subtlety of detail and in the addition of new forms, but does not undergo any significant modification or abandonment of early views; I shall therefore treat the account as a unit, noting changes and developments only in passing.

I *Pre-Capitalist Societies and the Notion of Class*

In the 1859 preface to *A Contribution to the Critique of Political Economy* Marx observes that "in broad outline, the Asiatic, ancient, feudal and modern bourgeois modes of production may be designated as epochs marking progress in the economic development of society."[6] This seems to be a view which he continues to hold throughout his career. It is these then, together with the protofeudal Germanic mode, which chiefly concern us here: Men, who were not in their earliest state settled but migratory, living by hunting, fishing or pastoralism, were nonetheless organized into relatively stable tribal communities, the tribe being their "natural common body" which "emerges from spontaneous evolution," as the family extends its ties through intermarriage.[7] This "natural" tribal organization is the precondition of the communal maintenance of life through labor, thus rendering "the first form of ownership . . . tribal ownership."[8] Only in that he is a member of the tribe does an individual see himself as owner of the land he uses. When men "finally settle down" the first form of property which they know is thus this tribal, communal property rather than private property—the term "property" here, as always in Marx, being limited to productive rather than strictly personal property such as the clothes one wears.[9]

Such a community of property "can realise itself in a variety of ways." At its most sophisticated in terms of economic development it is found in what Marx calls the Asiatic or Oriental mode or form.[10] In this form of property the communal ownership finds its expression in a despot who "may appear as the higher or *sole proprietor*," while the communities unified under his reign appear "only as hereditary possessors." From the Western viewpoint, but only from this viewpoint, their condition may even in some cases seem a kind of "general slavery." The despot, to be sure, as representative of the communal unity, takes—usually in the form of taxes—most of the surplus the community produces, since, the form being communal, no one producer has claim to it; a part may also go to the priesthood, as representatives and caretakers of the unity expressed religiously as "the imagined tribal entity of the god," while a final part may be stored communally as insurance against hard times.

Still, the relationship of the productive part of the community to the despot and his entourage and the priestly caste is not properly speaking, one of slavery; it is not in fact, properly speaking, a class relationship at all. For, though the relationship to the means of production—the demarcation which is usually taken to be the criterion for class membership in Marx—most certainly differs between these groups, this relationship is in reality a necessary condition for class formation only, not a sufficient one. What is lacking in the Asiatic form which would spur the development of social classes per se and the attendant dynamism that real class formation entails seems to be a division between town and country. The despot's city is a mere "princely camp, superimposed on the real economic structure" of society; it serves only as a trade center where the state's revenue is expended. The village, on the other hand, serves as the communal center for both agriculture and craft; there is thus no social division of labor between what we would regard as urban craft work and rural agriculturalism; the community in its work functions is unified; although specialization under such circumstances will necessarily be minimized, this holds true even in those cases where members of the community specialize in one kind of labor, specialists and nonspecialists alike, as the community, always functioning cooperatively in a unified whole.[11] Consequently, the communal form of property perseveres and survives indefinitely unless acted upon by external forces, that is, forces not endemic to the social relations of the form itself.[12] The Asiatic mode "necessarily survives longest and most stubbornly" compared to other social forms, since it does not spontaneously divide into warring classes and form the socially disruptive institutions of private property; whatever the particulars of its cultural development, the archaic form of tribal community and communal property survives in it intact. Strictly speaking, it has no history, at least in the sense that Marx uses the term in the *Manifesto*'s opening passage, viz., an internal, endemic, dynamic social movement leading to new socioeconomic forms.

This Asiatic mode comes itself in several varieties. Work may be communal or performed by individual families or it may involve both; its political organization, though ultimately lodged in the despot, may be more or less democratic at the village level. It is a mode which, as the name implies, finds for Marx its paradigm in Asian societies, especially those of China and precolonial India, which he knew best. But it was also the form of ancient Mesoamerica and Peru and the ancient Celtic communities of Europe. It was, he seems confident a decade after his original "Grundrisse" observations, in fact the initial form everywhere in Europe.[13]

If this is the case, one may be tempted to ask, how did these primeval sluggish communities ever develop into the Europe of the bourgeois epoch? In attempting to answer this question Marx admits that he has not complete data on hand, since one can only speculate on many details of the disruptions which led to the disintegration of the primal European communal forms. Migration and warfare seem the most likely culprits; in the case of classical civilization, which, in the form we find it in history, exhibits a mode which Marx calls the ancient, he suggests further that it did not reach its zenith, as, for example, India did, in the Asiatic (communal) mode since, there being less need for large-scale community projects such as extensive irrigation systems, the unity of the community in terms of communal

34   KARL MARX

property was less strongly reinforced.¹⁴ He also notes a mix-
ture of the Asiatic with new forms in several European communities—the Slavonic and Rumanian and the Russian—as well as
vestiges of it throughout most of Europe, indicating its tenacity
even in the face of drastic social change.

At any rate, whatever the dynamics, there emerges first in
southern Europe and much later in the forests of the north new
forms, the ancient and Germanic respectively. The development
of these and the eventual violent intercourse of the latter with
the ruins of the former will, as we have already noted above,
give rise to the feudal epoch which in its turn sets the stage for
capitalism.

The ancient mode which appears in Greece and Rome as well
as among the Jews and their neighbors is—unlike the Asiatic
where there is "a unity of town and country" and the village is
"a mere appendage to the land"—centered around a city with
its attached cultivated territory. It thus entails from the outset a
social division of labor beween town and country which ensures
a more dynamic internal development than can be the case in
the Asiatic mode. In the ancient form, however, in contrast to
the bourgeois mode with which we are familiar, it is the country
which dominates the city. Crafts and trading, the city occupations, are consequently universally held in low esteem and seen
as suitable occupations for freedmen and foreign migrants only;
full citizenship in neither Greece nor Rome was in general
granted to those who pursued such activities. In contrast, the
citizen is a free peasant who owns and cultivates his own plot,
though only in so far as he is a member of the city-state. Private
property and the division of labor emerge simultaneously in this
form. The right of citizenship is initially for the ancients synonymous with the right to hold land. Conversely, the responsibility
entailed by this citizenship is that of military service. This is
necessary in order to protect the community from outside
aggression but, *more importantly*, with an expanding population,
to secure *by aggression* the land guaranteed to each citizen.
Where several such city-states coexist this latter need, of course,
reinforces in turn the need for protection of the community and
so the two, interacting continually, produce an increasingly
great need for a strong military power. "War," says Marx, is

thus for the ancient form "the great all-embracing task, the great communal labor." The community is, as a result, organized along military lines.

The original tribal structures, from which the form grows, already embodied, as all but the simplest social organizations do, divisions of social status according to kinship group (clans or, as the Romans called them, *gens*); these divisions lent themselves nicely to the formation of a military hierarchy with the hierarch situated in the city proper. Thus, those *gentes* in Rome—the ancient society to which we, following Marx, will direct most of our attention—which came to be known as patrician, claiming descent from the fathers of the city, concentrated in the city and became the social and military directors of the society. As its administrative leadership, representing the community's unity, they originally enjoyed only the use of—although they later appropriated—all those public lands (*ager publicus*) which had not been given to citizens for cultivation, and worked them with tenant (client) and slave labor. Only the *gentes* of lower social status, the plebeians, could actually possess land, forming the soldier-farmer basis of the society in its original form; the amount each plebeian could possess was, however, strictly limited, a mere "compensation for a share in the common land."

This hierarchical military organization of society with its attendant warfare proved the downfall of the plebeian peasant farmers. As Marx put it, "the preservation of the ancient community implies the destruction of the conditions upon which it rests, and turns into its opposite." Conquest secured not only holdings for their children, but also slaves and an enlargement of the *ager publicus.* Hence the power of the patricians over the plebs increased as their "holdings," which were worked by slave labor, increased, finally supplanting plebeian peasant agriculture and rendering the plebs, a dispossessed urban "proletarian rabble."[15] This concentration of power was further intensified in Rome through a drop in demand for Italian grain, the peasantry's chief crop, due to the competition of "plundered and tribute-grain" from the conquered provinces; much of Italy was in the later years of the Empire organized into large estates on which cattle were grazed. In its full development then, ancient society relies on slavery as "the basis of the whole productive system."[16]

It arrives at this point, however, only in a condition of great tension, an expression of the "contradictory form of state landed property and private landed property" in the ancient world. In the Asiatic mode where we found a "unity of manufactures and agriculture," the need for "conquest is not so essential a condition as where *landed property, agriculture,* predominate exclusively." Hence slavery (as also serfdom) can never be anything but an adjunct to production in it. The Asiatic society, never developing a full social division of labor, can never develop true social classes as does ancient society, classes that must of necessity push the society to a breaking point from which emerges a dramatic, qualitative social change.

We have then at the zenith of ancient society three relatively well-formed classes: the patricians, the plebeians, and the slaves, the result of an expansionist system based upon the needs of agriculture. Of these three the slaves, despite sporadic uprisings, represent—presumably because of their necessary disorganization, a consequence of their condition of bondage—the last dynamic element, so much so that Marx can speak of the ancient class struggle as being limited to the freeborn rich and poor.[17] The plebeian class, though less limited, once reduced to the status of an urban proletariat, "owing to its intermediate position between propertied citizens and slaves, never achieved an independent development."[18] In a society in which country (land and agriculture) dominates city (crafts and trade) and "wealth as an end in itself appears [hence] only among a few trading peoples" who live in the "pores" of the society, it could not be transformed into an urban laboring class, which might have so developed. Marx usually characterizes the conditions under which a transformation of society can take place as marked by a conflict between old social relations and new processes of production which have rendered them obsolete; only when "existing social relations have come into contradiction with existing forces of production" does society undergo a significant change.[19] Here, though the past social relations were obviously made obsolete by the new wide-scale employment of slave labor, the plebs were not so much forced to change society along with themselves in virtue of the new productive processes as they were discarded by these processes. The plebeian proletariat was, consequently, never in a position to achieve a revolutionary transformation of Rome. It could not help but, nonetheless, undermine its stability, leaving Rome increasingly weakened before the forces of the equally expansionist German barbarians.[20] It is these we must examine next in piecing together Marx's account of the economic development of society.

The Germanic mode is a form which differs significantly from both the Asiatic, with its unity of town and country, and the ancient, with its "cities based on landownership and agriculture." Here we have a cultural form which begins "with the countryside as the locus of history." In it we find individual families as private owners of the land they till, but not exercising their private ownership, as among the ancients, through the medium of a city-state; with cities and usually even villages lacking, it is merely common culture and the existence of some common lands which preserves the community, "as an *association*, not as a *union*" or unity. This common land is, of course, thus—unlike the Roman *ager publicus*—not the state's in contrast to the individual's but truly commonly owned, consisting of woodlands and waste, which serve as hunting grounds, and common pasturage, that is, of all those lands which can only be communally used.

This form Marx apparently originally thought to be quite ancient, attributing its existence to the vast and largely unculivated German terrain "where single heads of families settle in the forests, separated by long distances." By 1881, however, he recognizes that in Julius Caesar's time nothing like it was present among the Germans, for land was then still divided among clans and tribes alone and cultivation was probably still communal.[21] A little over a hundred years later, in the time of Tacitus, it had undergone "a natural evolution" toward private ownership—a process Marx unfortunately fails to elaborate upon; but still the form remained basically communal, land being individually worked, although it was the property proper of the clan, which was usually settled together in a village. In the period of the Germanic migrations which toppled the Western Empire, this intermediate form disappears and we find the Ger-

manic mode per se introduced into all the countries which the
German tribes conquer. In its remnants of communalism, which
he now sees expressed in the persistence in medieval Europe of
common lands as well as private holdings, Marx finds the basis
of whatever "popular liberty and popular life" still remained in
the feudal Middle Ages. In its descentralization with the disappearance of most village communities—that is, its nearly
totally rural character—he finds the origins of the feudal epoch
with its characteristic dynamic opposition between countryside
and newly emerging towns.

Apparently it is the disruption caused by the migrations
themselves which gives the beginnings of feudal society its
rural nature. As early as 1845, when Marx was seemingly still
of the opinion that the rural Germanic mode antedated the
period of migrations, he and Engels still note in *The German
Ideology* that Western Europe was in this period far more
sparsely populated than it had been in the heyday of the
Empire.[22] For in the wake of the barbarian conquests agriculture,
industry, and trade had all decreased, with a consequent decline
in total population which "received no large increase from the
conquerors." Under such circumstances the natural isolation
which fosters the Germanic mode and which Marx originally
attributes to geographical factors, can be viewed as plausible
for quite different reasons.

The independent, isolated peasant could not for the most
part survive for long in the uncertain times of the migrations,
however, and the Germanic mode was—"under the influence of
the Germanic military constitution," the *comitatus* organization
of the German warrior bands—gradually superceded by the
feudal institution of serfdom.[23] This institution, though sharing
with slavery the use of a man as "an organic accessory of the
land," as just one more "among the natural conditions of production" for another, rather than as a member of a community,
differs from it greatly in particulars. The serf, unlike the slave,
cannot, under classical feudal conditions, be sold; though bound to
the land and forced to render the surplus he produces to the lord
who controls him, he can only be forced from it—an event which,
as we shall see, marks the breakup of the Middle Ages—if he
fails to meet his obligations to produce the desired surplus.

Serfdom replaces slavery as the condition of bondage in the society which emerges from the German conquest of Rome both because of particular historical reasons of the kind mentioned above and the aforementioned extreme decentralization of that society; the serf is as often as not made captive on a plot which he has formerly worked and to which he originally laid claim; there is, moreover, no state-controlled *ager publicus* or its equivalent readily at hand to which he can be bound in slavery—whatever public land exists in the Middle Ages is a remnant of an earlier communal form.[24]

The serfs, in their capacity *as* serfs, could, no more than the ancient slaves, exert a decisive influence *in itself* on the course of medieval history; this remained the case despite periodic rebellions that spoke of widespread dissatisfaction but "remained totally ineffective because of the isolation and consequent crudity of the peasants," both free and enserfed.[25] They could, however, as our account of the *Manifesto* suggested, do so in another capacity. Towns, for the most part not derived "ready-made from an earlier period" but newly emergent, or at the least reconstituted, began to appear, growing steadily as escaped serfs swarmed to them. These towns, due to numerous factors—the need for a military organization for self-protection in "the constant war" between town and country, the need of trade regulations as commerce flourished, the competition among the ever increasing number of escaped serfs, and the general feudal structure of society—developed a counterpart to the agricultural system in the guilds which formed the social basis of medieval manufacture. The guilds were organized according to craft, there being little or no division of labor within crafts; trade was, at least in the early years, carried on mainly by the guild masters themselves. The serfs, as they entered the towns, were either incorporated into the guild system or relegated to the position of casual day laborers. If the former, they were organized in a filial relation to their master which "suited the interests of the masters" and—contrary to the antagonism suggested in the *Manifesto* account—made for "real bond" between journeyman and master which was intensified by the journeymen's "interest in becoming masters themselves." Consequently, "journeymen never got further than small acts of insubordination within separate guilds, such as belong to the very nature of the guild."[26] On the other hand, as casual day laborers they remained an essentially "unorganized rabble" who, though they occasionally attempted revolts against the municipality, were basically impotent against the "organized power, armed for war" of the town fathers who were constantly "jealously watching over them."

Nevertheless, these towns of escaped serfs, organized as they were in their own hierarchies, in themselves as whole units provided an antagonism to the organization of the medieval countryside which was to prove the real dynamic in the development of feudal society. As among the ancients, where the town and country division, that is, the division of agricultural and urban craft labor, led—albeit following a circuitous path—to a society in which real social antagonisms emerged and effected social development, so also with the men of the Middle Ages. But, whereas the ancient city was based upon agriculture, the power of those who ruled it being derived from holdings in land, the medieval city was not. Starting from an entirely rural environment and developing explicitly in opposition to that environment, it could achieve an antagonistic independence of the agricultural social order which the ancient cities never could. The artisan was no longer suspect; craft, in fact, enjoyed high prestige and its development was encouraged. The towns might be exploited politically by the countryside, but they in turn were able to exploit it economically.[27] Commerce develops everywhere in which we find a division of labor between town and country, since the town must sell its products to the countryside and purchase its food from it; and commerce in its turn tends to develop the towns. Still, among the ancients such urban development never led to significant developments in manufacture as it did, as we shall presently see, in the late medieval world.[28]

Before turning to this account of the rise of capitalism, however, let me here summarize our findings so far on the relationship of history to class struggle. History, as we have seen, is for Marx in its primary and most interesting sense not simply a series of temporally ordered events in the social world but a movement intrinsic to societies which leads to radically new social forms. In this movement accident can most certainly play a role, just as it might also in the movement of an ahistorical community to the beginnings of historical development; thus, to give one example, the externally necessitated migrations of the Germans is both the immediate cause of the end of Roman history and the source of a new, potentially historical Germanic social form.[29] The primary determinants of historical movement are, however, the antagonistic components which form, so to speak, the body of the movement. These components—or, to use Hegelian terminology, moments of the dialectical process— need not be social classes themselves or even, at least directly, expressions of the interaction of classes. In Roman society we do see patricians and plebians developing in classes through an interaction grounded in their different property forms (the "contradiction" between state and private landed property); in this struggle, however, large-scale slavery develops as a patrician institution pitting the patrician/slave complex, not itself a social class but a unity of two classes (themselves in opposition), against the plebs. Since the patricians are obviously the rulers in this complex, we might, in this case, ultimately rest content with a description in terms of an opposition between patricians and plebs alone. In feudal society, however, the role of class interaction is even more clearly indirect. Primarily, the antagonism is one between town and country—the lord/serf complex in opposition to the hierarchical association of the towns; the internal antagonism of the relation between lord and serf, of course, provides the *impetus* for this opposition and will, as we shall see, be resolved *in* it, but what ultimately confront each other are not classes per se.[30] Thus any textbook account of Marx's class struggle in terms of simple triads with classes as the simple moments of these triads will have to be abandoned; both the moments and the patterns of dialectical development in Marx are far too complex for such an analysis. For him, as for his great predecessor Hegel, the real pattern of the dialectic is far more subtle than that which the thesis-antithesis-synthesis form suggests.

A brief general account of the complex relationship between class, division of labor, and private property in the material presented above also seems in order here. As I have already indicated, the formation of classes is for Marx a development of the same process which begins with a certain type of division of labor, but the division of labor is itself a phenomenon which covers such a variety of instances that it needs further explication as well. The simplest and first split in labor function is for Marx and Engels "the division of labour in the sexual act" and that caused generally "by virtue of natural predisposition."[31] Based upon these factors there is they further say, "a natural division of labor in the family and the separation of society into individual families opposed to one another." This need not, as we have seen in Marx's account of Asiatic society, develop into either institutions of private property or what I have called a social division of labor, that is, a labor division in which individuals no longer function socially or cooperatively as a social unity, a situation which is exemplified in the division of labor between agriculture and craft in the town/country opposition. It is also not necessary that such a social division of labor appear simultaneously with private property, as the example of the Germanic mode attests. Only with institutions of private property in existence, however, can a social division of labor emerge. The town/country bifurcation is thus present both in the ancient and the feudal forms and can *develop from* the Germanic form, but does not appear spontaneously in the Asiatic where community of property still obtains; this community of property exists, of course, only insofar as the unity of village organization prevents the emergence of a social division of labor, but the breakdown of village unity manifests itself invariably as the emergence of private property either accompanied by or chronologically prior to a social division of labor; the former appears to be the case in the ancient mode—though Marx never really discusses its origins—while the latter is definitely the pattern of development in the passage from the Germanic protofeudal to the feudal mode itself.

II *The Development of Capitalist Society*

There exists at the end of the Middle Ages for the first time in history what Marx considers the three preconditions for the development of industrial capitalism: First, there are large numbers of "free" laborers, free "in the double sense that neither they themselves form part and parcel of the means of production, as in the case of slaves, bondsmen, etc., nor do the means of production belong to them, as in the case of peasant proprietors."[32] These laborers, separated as they are from their labor's "material prerequisite" in that they are separated from the land, both land of their own and their master's, are ultimately obliged to sell their "labor power," that is, their power to work, thus providing the army of wage laborers on which capitalism depends.[33] Second, there is a considerable mass of capital at hand, both usurer's capital and—far more important—merchant capital, due to the great development of trade which accompanies and in turn spurs the growth of towns in the late Middle Ages. Still, these two preconditions by themselves—a proletariat and large quantities of commercial capital—existed previously in the latter days of the ancient world. And yet neither the advent of the capitalist form of free wage labor nor the process of industrialization ever took place. Instead, the ancient world was merely transformed from "a patriarchal system devoted to the production of immediate means of subsistence into one devoted to the production of surplus-value (i.e., saleable goods)," the ancient's surplus itself being largely agricultural and largely produced by traditional technological means.[34] Another factor or factors must thus be introduced to explain the difference between late medieval conditions and those of Rome at the height of its development. Marx believes he has discovered the source of this difference in the independent development of the medieval towns. For, whereas urban craft in ancient society was always so subordinated to landed property that its development was relatively insignificant, the place it occupied in the independent medieval town was such that it was able to develop to the point where it "had out-grown the guild system" which henceforth proved a great "embarrassment" to it.[35]

This development begins with "the separation of production and commerce" in the medieval towns, a legacy from Roman times in the towns that had survived the barbarian migrations but a practice before long adopted also in the newly formed municipalities.[36] Once this occurs and commerce becomes the "prerogative of a particular class," it is extended over wider areas, resulting in "a new division of production between the individual towns, each of which is soon exploiting a predominant branch of industry." The outcome of such specialization is the beginning of the previously alluded to "manufacture," which appears first in Southern Europe in Italy as early as the fourteenth or fifteenth century and somewhat later in the north of Europe in Flanders. By the sixteenth century it exists throughout much of Western Europe. It is the first form of capitalist production and will continue to be the dominant form "from the middle of the 16th to the last third of the 18th century."[37]

In this system of production no novel technological innovations are employed; we find simply that labor has been made more efficient both through centralization—a large number of workers being concentrated in one spot or under one director for a single purpose—and through a significant increase in the division of labor. The tendency toward centralization appears first. As Marx says, "manufacture, in its strict meaning, is hardly to be distinguished, in its earliest stages, from the handicraft trades of the guilds, otherwise than by the greater number of workmen simultaneously employed by one and the same individual capital. The workshop of the mediaeval master handicraftsman is simply enlarged."[38] This enlargement in itself, however, soon leads to a division of labor: "An increased quantity of the article [being produced] has perhaps to be delivered within a given time. The work is therefore re-distributed. Instead of each man being allowed to perform all the various operations in succession, these operations are changed into disconnected, isolated ones carried on side by side; each is assigned to a different artificer, and the whole of them together are performed simultaneously by the co-operating workmen."[39] Gradually, this practice "ossifies into a systematic division of labour." Alternatively, we might find a number of handicraftsmen with differing skills together employed in the production of a single product which requires the skill of each of them—Marx uses the example of the production of a carriage by the combined efforts of wheelwrights, harnessmakers, tailors, locksmiths, etc. Gradually, once again the craftsman "being now exclusively occupied in carriage-making ... loses, through want of practice, the ability to carry on, to its full extent, his old handicraft." Carriage-making is split up "into its various detail processes" and the new division of labor is complete. The commodity is now "the social product of a union of artificers" each of whom possesses a very partial and detailed skill.

Such manufacture increases productive efficiency for the entrepreneur in a number of ways, even without the introduction of machinery. The sheer fact of cooperation of a large number of laborers in itself tends to save costs both in outlay for physical plant and, in some cases, even for tools, while it flattens out the differences in efficiency between laborers, making the capitalist less dependent on the energies of any particular individual or individuals. Moreover, according to Marx, man being a social animal, the very fact that cooperation fosters "social contact begets in most industries an emulation and a stimulation of the animal spirits that heighten the efficiency of each individual workman."[40] The new division of labor, on the other hand, diminishes the costs of training workers and allows for the increased skill of further specialization.[41] It also tends in itself to increase efficiency: "The habit of doing only one thing converts [the worker] into a never failing instrument, while his connection with the whole mechanism compels him to work with the regularity of the parts of a machine."

Only where conditions for this new mode of production were already forming within the Middle Ages does it appear and develop. Thus, for example, the existence of large quantities of merchants' capital in Portugal does nothing to aid its development in manufacturing, while Holland becomes the foremost capitalist nation of the seventeenth century. Though the revolutions in commerce of the sixteenth and seventeenth centuries "constitute one of the principal elements in furthering the transition from feudal to capitalist mode of production," these revolutions themselves were "accomplished conversely on the basis of the already existing capitalist mode of production." The world market may form the foundation for this productive mode, but its tendency to expand production "tends to extend the world-market continually, so that it is not commerce in this case which revolutionises industry, but industry which revolutionises commerce."[42]

We have already examined (in our discussion of the *Manifesto* in the first section of this chapter) the factors—aside from the development of industry—which fostered the development and eventual revolution in commerce. A question remains, however, as to how the laborers of the Middle Ages became a "free" proletariat when, in the framework of feudal society, they were, in the countryside, either largely tied to feudal lords or semi-independent and independent peasants while, in the towns, they were constantly under the sway of the guilds. In Marx's account of this transition we see for the first time clearly the proletarian partisan within him emerging to stand behind the shoulder of the dispassionate historian, using the full power of his irony to express an outrage which cannot help but sweep the reader along with it at the rank injustice of these events.[43] For here we see the direct ancestors of the modern proletarians for whom he is writing, finally having broken the shackles of feudal bondage, only to be bound again as "free" laborers, by the subtler shackles of the wage.

Wherever capitalism appears, Marx tells us, "the abolition of serfdom has been long effected." It was thus not capitalism which accomplished this task. Rather it was the growth of commerce within feudal society itself. As commerce developed between town and countryside the serf was often able to buy exemptions from various manorial obligations with money obtained on surplus which he sold; this practice was, moreover, frequently encouraged by the lords themselves who—also increasingly involved in a monetary commercial economy—began to prefer cash to feudal service; thus reinforced, it became more widespread over time until finally the serf/lord relationship had for all practical purposes disappeared.[44] Thus the growth of commerce enabled the serfs to accomplish what their own struggle never could have; and, first in Italy, and then in Northern Europe in the Lowlands and England by the last part of the fourteenth century, serfdom had "practically disappeared."

It was not, however, replaced by a world of propertyless proletarians begging for employment, but by a world of independent or semi-independent propertied peasants, far better off than they had ever previously been; a kind of "golden age" for the yeomanry of Europe—especially those of England where prosperity and independence reached a zenith—was commencing on the eve of what Marx, quoting William Thornton's "Overpopulation and Its Remedy," calls the "iron age" to come. This newly emancipated peasantry was about to be emancipated from the land. Marx traces the history of this expropriation largely in England where it takes its "classic form," but it happened elsewhere as well—in Scotland, in France, in the Lowlands and Italy—as his observations attest. Beginning in the last third of the fifteenth century it continues, in one form or another, far into the modern period. Its prelude in England is the breaking up of the bands of feudal retainers who had outlived the feudal era, a move which the crown, "itself a product of bourgeois development," precipitated in its pursuit of absolute sovereignty. The feudal lords themselves, however, initiated the era of peasant expropriation—in opposition to both king and parliament—by seizing the common lands and the lands of their former serfs quite illegally, via bogus interpretations of already obsolete relationships, in order to turn them into sheep walks to provide wool for the newly developed wool manufactures of Flanders. Marx quotes Thomas More in his *Utopia* as saying that in England the sheep, formerly "so meke and tame," now "eate up, and swallow downe, the very men themselfes." Laws, apparently time and again, were enacted against such enclosures during the reigns of both Henry VII and Henry VIII, but they had no real effect. The coming of the Reformation to England during the latter, moreover, hastens the process of expropriation, for the Catholic church, which lost its property in this period, was "feudal proprietor of a great part of the English land." The confiscated church lands were for the most part "given away to rapacious royal favorites, or sold at a nominal price to speculating farmers and citizens, who drove out, *en masse*, the hereditary sub-tenants and threw their holdings into one." Whatever the crown's benevolent feelings for its yeomanry, its actions in their real effect often belie them; there was money to be made in enclosure and the new commercial acquisitiveness could hardly be stopped. With the church no longer functional, its monastics were also proletarianized. Pauperism was becoming a widespread phenomenon in England; in Elizabeth's reign it was recognized as such in law.

The yeomanry even in Cromwell's time were still numerous, however. By 1750, though, they had disappeared. The Stuart restoration saw the landed gentry secure by legal means all further usurpation—at the same time establishing modern title to their land. With the Revolution of 1688, power is in the joint hands of the landlords and capitalists with the result that the crown's land, that is, state land, follows the same sad history as the peasant holdings. In Scotland, after the defeat of Bonnie Prince Charlie at Culloden, the Scottish clan lords turn landlord and drive their people off the land in order to make room for the sheep. In the eighteenth century, seizure of what common land remains is secured through the law. Force began the process; with the bourgeoisie and its allies now in power the means, however, become more refined.[45] By all of these "idyllic methods of primitive accumulation" of capital, writes Marx, "they conquered the field for capitalist agriculture, made the soil part and parcel of capital, and created for the town industries the necessary supply of a 'free' and outlawed proletariat."

But this proletariat, especially when—in the late fifteenth and sixteenth century—it was newly created, was not readily willing to throw itself on the ill-demonstrated mercy of the labor market; nor could the budding manufacturing enterprises fully absorb it as yet. Consequently, the proletarians "were turned *en masse* into beggars, robbers, vagabonds, partly from inclination, [but] in most cases from stress of circumstances." The state for its part responded with some of the cruelest legislation in history; flogging, branding, even execution—in the case of repeating offenders—are the standard prescriptions for vagabondage; slavery, long extinct in Europe, is reintroduced to combat the menace as well. By the seventeenth century the problem appears also in France; the cure here too is equally severe. "Thus," writes Marx, "were the agricultural people, first forcibly expropriated from the soil, driven from their homes, turned into vagabonds, and then whipped, branded, tortured by laws grotesquely terrible, into the discipline necessary for the wage system." For all through this period manufactures has been growing as well—roughly in proportion to this subjugation of the new labor force in fact. The original wage laborers of the fourteenth century, few in numbers and situated in a social setting which strengthened their position, could extract reasonably high wages; in contrast, the growing proletariat—blocked from a life of vagabondage—was increasingly at the mercy of capital. "Factories," observes Marx, "like the royal navy, recruited by the press gang."

Once driven into the shops, the process of discipline continues. In the early years of capitalism, before a working class which accepts "the conditions of the [capitalist] mode of production as self-evident laws of Nature" has been formed, and the virtues of free enterprise can be extolled, force is everywhere very much in evidence and the power of the state is used to regulate wages and the length of the working day.[46] As early as 1349 in England statutes setting maximum wages and a minimum working day are enacted;[47] unions of laborers are at the same time forbidden. These laws remain in effect until the beginning of the nineteenth century when they either had become anomalous or were stricken down by parliament "under the pressure of the masses." In France and the Netherlands the situation is again much the same. Even at the beginning of the French Revolution the newly won right to union organization is revoked; the law which revokes it is not itself repealed until over half a century later. The sycophants of the bourgeoisie seem in unanimous agreement on the value of creating an "absolute dependence" of the wage workers; a "degraded and almost servile condition of the mass of the people" was especially important to capitalism in its infancy, both for the purpose of accumulation of capital and the establishment of capitalist work relations between employer and employed.

The expropriation of the peasantry had additional benefits for capitalism in that it created a home market for both agricultural and manufactured goods which the dispossessed had formerly grown and produced for themselves.[48] Improved methods in agriculture, a result in part of the increased commerce in agricultural products in the late Middle Ages, enabled the same or even increased production to be maintained despite the smaller number of producers in the wake of expropriation; the gradual conversion of agriculture to the capitalist mode of organization improved productivity even more; thus, the same forces which gave the peasant a moment of independence at the end of the Middle Ages were creating the agricultural revolution which would enable it soon to be taken away. Ex-

propriation, moreover, formed a wedge whereby early manufacture obtained its initial grasp on the European economy.
Though manufacture first arose in the Northern Italian cities
and was based largely on export trade, it established itself
most often in its early history in the countryside in villages
where there was no resistance from the guilds, basing itself
on simple rural industries, such as spinning and weaving—the
crafts which were formerly, before expropriation, plied domestically in the peasant home. The subsumption of more highly
skilled urban craft in general followed later—usually through
the economic destruction of the guilds, only infrequently through
their transformation into capitalist enterprises. This initial destruction of the old economic order having occurred in the
countryside, the entire countryside is from the first involved
in the new system of production. Town may dominate country
in the new order, but it is with power first developed in the
country that the town is itself transformed. "The ancients,"
writes Marx, "who never advanced beyond specifically urban
craft skill and application, were never able to achieve large-
scale industry."[49] The integration of the countryside into an
urban dominated order based on commerce and industry is
apparently necessary for such a project.[50]

In the meantime in the New World—Africa having been
turned into "a warren for the commercial hunting of black-
skins"—a system of slavery was developing which served as
"a pedestal" for the "veiled slavery of the wage-workers in
Europe."[51] The Dutch practiced a similar system in Java. And
everywhere a developing colonial system plundered the local
populations. In the mother country the system of public credit,
that is, the national debt, at the same time plundered the new
wage workers who were taxed to pay the state creditors, a
practice which Marx cites Jan De Witt as lauding because it
produced a worker who was "submissive, frugal, industrious
and overburdened with labour." It also had the virtue—from
the capitalist perspective—of further dispossessing the peasantry
as well as numerous artisans. "Over-taxation," Marx observes,
"is not an incident, but rather a principle" in the bourgeois
world.

A full account of the effects of the introduction of machinery into the capitalist system must—dependent as it is on an exposition of the labor theory of value—await the discussion of *Capital* in Chapter 6; in fact, a full account of the dynamics of the capitalist class struggle—of the dynamics of capitalism per se— can only be presented in the light of this theory. Nevertheless, I shall try here to present something of an account of capitalist development, both in order to complete our account of the history of the economic development of society as seen by Marx and to present an introduction to the later discussion of Chapter 6. Machinery, which first makes its appearance on a large-scale in England during the latter third of the eighteenth century, effected considerable changes in both the organization and nature of work for the proletarians; in fact, it even significantly altered the constitution of the work force itself. For as— due to the intervention of machinery—strength became less essential to a variety of productive processes, the scope of female and child labor increased; the family as a whole now becomes a laboring family to an even greater extent than in the period of manufacture—without, however, an attendant increase in income, as the price of labor generally drops in proportion to this change; the resistance of the male operatives to capital's demands which had developed during the period of manufacture is likewise undermined.[52] This was especially disastrous to labor in view of the fact that the increased dependence on machinery gave capital an incentive to both lengthen the working day and intensify labor. The former arises from the fact that the new machinery is "an industrial *perpetuum mobile*, that would go on producing forever, did it not meet with certain natural obstacles in the weak bodies and the strong wills of its human attendants." It is especially strong in the period of transition from manufacture when monopolistic conditions produce windfall profits for the new industrialists in a field. Resistance to this lengthened day "is moreover lessened by the apparent lightness of machine work, and by the more pliant and docile character of the women and children employed on it." The latter, namely, intensification of labor, is a direct consequence of machine production itself; as skills become simpler and operatives grow accustomed to the machine they attend to, rapidity and intensity tend to increase. This situation is further aggravated when pressure from labor halts the increase in working time. Thus, in England, as soon as Parliament was forced in the mid-nineteenth century to set a normal working day through pressure from labor, the capitalist class, by "hastening on the further improvement of machinery," attempted to secure more work from labor in the time that it was allowed. Hence, it should be noted, not only intracapitalist rivalry but the force of labor itself spurs on the revolutionary development of the means of production, which we spoke of earlier in our account of the *Manifesto;* moreover, as labor's power increases, it becomes an increasingly powerful force to this end.

In general one finds an almost stupendous deterioration in working conditions as modern industrialism develops, a tendency which seems to have suffered few significant setbacks from Marx's day to the present—this despite legislation which he adequately demonstrates was both inadequate, since it served the interests as much of capital as of labor, and as difficult to enforce in his own time as in ours. The factory was unhealthy and unsafe, and the work was, moreover, far more boring than during the manufacturing period; the modern factory operative is compared by Marx, quoting Engels, to Sisyphus, condemned by the gods to a repetitive futile task. "At the same time that factory work exhausts the nervous system to the uttermost," he writes, "it does away with the many-sided play of the muscles, and confiscates every atom of freedom, both in bodily and intellectual activity. The lightening of the labour, even, becomes a sort of torture, since the machine does not free the labourer from work, but deprives the work of all interest." Moreover, the introduction of machinery into the work process destroyed all manufacture and handicraft industries it invaded, displacing the workmen in them. The combination of this fact with the above created for the first time a situation in which the workers fought against not simply their capitalist employers, but the means of production itself. Through both legal means and direct action, labor, from the seventeenth century until the beginning of the nineteenth, tried to halt the advent of machine production. It was only with "time and experience," says Marx, that "the workpeople learnt to distinguish between machinery and its employment by capital, and to direct their attacks, not against the material instruments of production, but against the mode in which they are used."

For the machine is, under capitalism, a "competitor of the workman." It may, as it did in the case of the English hand-loom weavers confronted by the powerloom, reduce overnight the value of a craft or detail skill, making instant paupers of its practitioners.[53] The constant tendency of industrial capitalism to revolutionize the productive means, that is, to introduce more efficient machinery, makes the threat of such displacement, moreover, constant. The growth of capitalist enterprise may, of course, reabsorb a part of the work force so displaced—though seldom immediately and usually at the lower wages of less skilled work—but this merely leaves the working people "continually both repelled and attracted" by modern industry. Those employed, furthermore, being constantly open to replacement at lower wages by the "industrial reserve army" of the unemployed are more easily disciplined by capital. "When capital enlists science into her service," Marx quotes Andrew Ure as writing, "the refractory hand of labour will always be taught docility." This industrial reserve army, in its turn, will, over time, according to Marx, tend to outstrip the reabsorption of laborers through capitalist growth.[54]

All of these factors, combined with the previously discussed periodicity of modern capitalist production—"the life of modern industry" becoming "a series of periods of moderate activity, prosperity, over-production, crisis and stagnation"—lead to a chronic and intensifying antagonism between labor and capital. Industrial capital, on the one hand, has developed the means of production far beyond the dreams of past forms; on the other, it produces a misery and insecurity which are difficult to endure. When—as we shall see on Marx's view it must—it gradually decreases in its rate of development of the social productive forces, so that it becomes in this respect a hindrance rather than a help as well, its death knell will be sounded; its sole *raison d'etre* having been undermined, the forces of its antagonist, one way or another, must bring it down.

In terms of work organization, industrial production tends to be simpler than that of manufacture; for division of labor in the factory is "primarily a distribution of the workmen among specialized machines; and of masses of workmen, not however organized into groups, among the various departments of the factory, in each of which they work at a number of similar machines placed together."[55] It does, however, introduce a new division of labor in its creation of "a superior class of workmen, some of them scientifically educated"—the technical work force which is "distinct from the factory operative class and merely aggregated to it."[56] What manufacture and machine production share in organization is the fundamental organization of capitalism itself—that is, the wage as central to the relationship between capital and labor, the laborer as "free," selling his labor power as any other commodity on the market— unlike the slave and serf whose labor power is treated by their masters as a natural resource akin to land or water or air. Labor, the modern proletariat, also—unlike its slave and serf predecessors—is able to form an independent organization of struggle against its oppressors, the first "independent movement of the immense majority, in the interests of the immense majority" in history.[57]

CHAPTER 3

Marx on Communist Society

IN speaking of the Paris Commune in *The Civil War in France,* Marx says of the workers among the communards: "They have no ready-made utopias to introduce by decree of the people. . . . They have *no ideals* to realize, but to set free the elements of the new society with which the old collapsing bourgeois society is pregnant." He might just as easily—even more easily perhaps—have said this of himself.[1] The form which the future communist society will take must for him be worked out in the everyday politics of the class struggle. The utopian socialists' "fantastic pictures of future society" were produced at a time when proletarian organization was embryonic and are totally inappropriate to an era of proletarian maturity.[2] Even in their heyday in fact their real function was largely only the negative, critical one of providing an attack on the principles of existing society; thereafter they tend to become, if anything, reactionary. For they substitute their own fantastical programs for the reality of class struggle, diverting attention from it or even presenting an opposition to the proletariat's engagement in it, the Owenites and the Fourierists respectively opposing the proletarian movements of the Chartists in England and the Reformistes in France. "In proportion as the modern class struggle develops and takes definite shape," writes Marx, the utopians' speculations and proposals "lose all practical value and all theoretical justification."[3] As a theoretician of scientific rather than utopian socialism his task is to provide an understanding of the social processes that lead to social transformations, not to legislate their outcomes in the manner of a moralist; as a practical politician it is to coordinate the proletariat's struggle for power. Consequently, in the few places where he does speak of the nature of communist society, he usually limits himself to those few general features which he feels confident must be present of necessity in view of the history which a communist social organization—founded on a workers' revolution—must have. The transitional workers' state, which he sees as a necessary step for both the abolition of classes and the consequent abolition of the state, receives a somewhat more extensive—that is, detailed—treatment, but only because it is an element of political practice, thus making its treatment invariably political and practical rather than directly theoretical.[4] Marx, that is to say, never intends these observations on the revolutionary political and social organization to be viewed as a fixed model for all times and places; they are remarks on immediate political questions only and are hardly to be taken seriously as proposals twenty, much less a hundred years after they were made, a fact which Marxist ideologues, viewing Marxism as ideology rather than scientific theory accompanied by an attendant practice, are incapable of understanding—a failing which often lends a comical quaintness to their views.

Remarks on the nature of communist society are found scattered throughout most of Marx's writings. In the *1844 Manuscripts* it is described as not only "positive abolition of *private property*" but also the abolition of "human self-alienation" and hence "the real *appropriation* of *human* nature," that is, "humanism."[5] It is, says Marx, "the *definitive* resolution of the antagonism between man and Nature, and between man and man." Nature has "*human* significance" only in communist society in that only under the conditions of free cooperative activity for the purpose of appropriating nature and using it for the satisfaction of social needs does nature provide the basis for a bond between men; in class society, on the contrary, there is struggle over the fruits of nature and hence nature forms the basis for human antagonism. Again, communism is here for Marx "the true solution of the conflict . . . between individual and species." For only in communism is the power of the species developed through cooperation between individuals rather than as a result of their competitive conflict; social cooperation is, of course, far from nonexistent in precommunist forms, but only in communism is one's every productive act understood as a social act—that is, an act in relation to society. In fact, even one's *"own existence* is a social activity" in communist society; consequently, "what I myself produce I produce for society, and with the consciousness of acting as a social being."

The bifurcation of interests between the individual and society, like the division of society into social classes itself, has its origin ultimately in the division of labor. Marx also believes that it will only be eliminated via the abolition of the division of labor. This, he says in *The German Ideology,* is itself only possible in the context of communism as well as itself being necessary for the full development of communism.[6] Thus the antagonism between town and country which results from a social division of labor between the two must be abolished as "one of the first conditions of communal life."[7] Beyond the abolition of this division—what Marx at one point calls "the greatest division of material and mental labour"—there is for him, moreover, the necessity as well as the inevitability of abolishing the division of labor per se under communism. In a somewhat bucolic-sounding passage, which has of late often been wrongly understood as advocacy of rural communalism on the countercultural model, he states that, whereas in capitalist society and class society generally a man "is a hunter, a fisherman, a shepherd, or a critical critic, and must remain so if he does not want to lose his means of livelihood ... in communist society, where nobody has one exclusive sphere of activity but each can become accomplished in any branch he wishes, society regulates the general production and thus makes it possible for me to do one thing today and another tomorrow, to hunt in the morning, fish in the afternoon, rear cattle in the evening, criticize after dinner, just as I have a mind, without ever becoming hunter, fisherman, shepherd or critic."[8]

Why Marx feels that this must happen may not be immediately apparent in view of the fact that, as we saw, division of labor within the family and according to sex as well as that based upon natural skill seems to be compatible with communal social organization insofar as it coexists with it in primitive communalistic forms. It becomes clearer, however, when we note that Marx does not anticipate anything like the traditional organization of the family in *modern* communist society. The proletarian family of the nineteenth century was at best a tenuous entity itself—in practice, nonexistent, writes Marx in the *Communist Manifesto*—and the sexual division of labor had already been undermined by the needs and new techniques of capital; the patriarchal family unit could thus easily be seen as already obsolete in the era of modern industry. Furthermore, a person is in no way precluded from making extensive use of a natural talent in the society Marx envisions; he simply believes that a variety of such talents will emerge once they are encouraged to do so. For modern communist society for the first time opens up the full range of potential for a person to develop "his gifts in all directions," creating a true "personal freedom" as opposed to what has passed for personal freedom up until this point—namely, the "right to the undisturbed enjoyment, upon certain conditions, of fortuity and chance," the "certain conditions" being "the productive forces and forms of intercourse at any particular time." Primitive communism, with its parochial institutions and relatively crude technology, could never provide this full scope of possibilities, but once available to a knowledgeable, self-controlling mankind it will, Marx feels, surely be exploited as fully as it possibly can.[9]

The theme of the abolition of the division of labor—contrary to the views of some writers, e.g., the sociologist Lewis Feuer —does not vanish from Marx's later thought. However, when it appears in *Capital* its necessity is presented in terms of the needs of modern industry rather than either those of modern communal organization per se or the individual free communist man. The constant development of modern industry necessitates, Marx observes, a flexible work force capable of a variety of functions, while capitalist organization of industry "reproduces the old division of labour with its ossified particularisations."[10] This failure of capitalist organization is inevitable, moreover, not only because capitalism is predicated on a "social anarchy," which Marx feels it cannot escape, but also because it has the previously mentioned need to maintain an industrial reserve army, the existence of which is more easily maintained in the absence of a flexible work force. The division of labor is both intrinsic to capitalism and obsolete. Its abolition is thus necessary on the grounds of the nature of the dynamics of modern industry alone; also, happily, however, it coincides with the need of humans for a full development:[11] "Modern industry, indeed, compels society under penalty of death, to replace the detail worker of today, crippled by life-long repetition of one and the same trivial operation, and thus reduced to the mere fragment of a man, by the fully developed individual, fit for a variety of labours, ready to face any change of production, and to whom the different social functions he performs, are but so many modes of giving free scope to his own natural and acquired powers." The concept of true "personal freedom" which we found in *The German Ideology*—however we ultimately choose to view its relation to communism at this point—seems still to be very much in evidence twenty-one years later.

It would, however, be incorrect to assume that this is all that personal freedom amounts to in Marx. Labor, even that form of labor which gives "free scope" to our powers, is—despite the fetishism of labor which we find in today's so-called communist countries, which began their "socialist" careers in a technologically backward state and were thus forced to rapidly accumulate capital by way of superexploitation of labor—never made a fetish by Marx. Although in the *Critique of the Gotha Program* he does speak of labor becoming, in the final stages of communism, "life's prime want," the term as used here carries a very different sense than it normally does when we are dealing with forced wage or bound labor. For, in roughly the same period, he writes in the third volume of *Capital*:[12]

In fact, the realm of freedom actually begins only where labour which is determined by necessity and mundane considerations ceases; thus in the very nature of things it lies beyond the sphere of actual material production. Just as the savage must wrestle with Nature to satisfy his wants, to maintain and reproduce life, so must civilised man, and he must do so in all social formations and under all possible modes of production. With his development this realm of physical necessity expands as a result of his wants; but, at the same time, the forces of production which satisfy these wants also increase. Freedom in this field can only consist in socialised man, the associated producers, rationally regulating their interchange with Nature, bringing it under their common control, instead of being ruled by it as by the blind forces of Nature; and achieving this with the least expenditure of energy and under conditions most favourable to, and worthy of, their human nature. *But it nonetheless still remains a realm of necessity.* Beyond it begins that development of human energy which is an end in itself, *the true realm of freedom,* which, however, can blossom forth only with this realm of necessity as its basis. The shortening of the working-day is its basic prerequisite.

The scope of the "realm of necessity" will, it should be noted, itself be socially decided in communist society—society itself must democratically decide what its wants are, what its living standard is to be, at any given time. Having decided this and arranged for the minimal expenditure of work time under socially acceptable conditions to secure it, the remainder of individuals' time is leisure, though it seems safe to speculate that it will not necessarily look much like what we—far more burdened by toil in a system of wage labor—consider leisure.[13] On the whole, it should prove to involve less intoxication to oblivion and less passive recreation; though this is not to say that both intoxication and passivity may not still have their place. Nonetheless, the prototype of activity in the "realm of freedom" is more likely to be that of the hobby, though "hobbies" now, rather than being limited to somewhat eccentric and introverted minor projects, are just as likely to involve huge and socially useful efforts of social cooperation voluntarily undertaken—the exploration of space, mutual education in the arts, the production of drama and films, scientific research, etc.— as well as the craft production of those entities, not deemed of social necessity, which cannot be adequately produced by machine.

With the disappearance of the antagonism between the individual and society resulting from the abolition of social classes, the state, as already noted, itself will disappear. For, being in actuality "the combination of one class over against another," it is, as Marx puts it in *The German Ideology,* "not only a completely illusory community, but a new fetter as well."[14] So long as "natural" conditions govern our productive life and social cooperation remains, so to speak, a natural accident in the unfolding of the historical development of human production, the real origins of social power in social cooperation will not be apparent, while the real natural conflict in class society will at the same time cry out for *"practical* intervention and control." Hence, the state arises as an "illusory 'general interest'" which masks its real role as a means of stabilization for the continuation of power of a dominant class; every ruling class, that is to say, in order to rule must "conquer for itself political power in order to represent its interest... as the general interest" via the institution of the state.[15] This is not to say, however, that state power is usually, if ever, the simple imposition of ruling class desires, irrespective totally of the needs and wishes of the dominated classes; to see it as such is to fail to see the class struggle reflected in it—thus, ultimately, to fail to take seriously the theory of class struggle;[16] the interest of the ruling class is presented as the general interest via the state only insofar as decisions, taking into account the class struggle, always presuppose the social and economic dominance of the class that rules. With, however, the disappearance of class and class rule and the substitution for it of a true communal association, "public power will lose [this] its political character."[17] The state will have been superceded by the reality of which it is a distorted image; the wage system will suffer the same fate. In the full development of communist society, the socialist slogan "From each according to his ability, to each according to his needs!" can at last be realized.[18]

But none of these above developments can appear as it were overnight. To understand how Marx thinks they can and will develop out of the conditions of modern society, we must turn to his observations on the transitional rule of the proletariat, communist society, "not as it has *developed* on its own foundations but... just as it *emerges* from capitalist society... economically, morally, and intellectually, still stamped with the birthmarks of the old society from whose womb it emerges."[19] The proletariat, Marx claims in *The German Ideology*, is the first class in history which, having the ability to secure power, can—once power has been obtained—accomplish the abolition of classes; this is due to the fact that it has no "particular class interest to assert against the ruling class."[20] It has, that is to say, no vested property interests, being a propertyless class, so that it consequently will not be burdened by any of the attendant social

relations (class relations) which accompanied the property interests of previous ruling classes; its only recourse, therefore, on taking power is to abolish the private property which it finds in
existence, reducing all of society to its own condition—that is,
making the entire society a proletariat and the development of
the proletariat thus the development of society. This development
should necessarily enhance the "free development" of individuals
as, unlike the members of past ruling classes, the proletarians are
of necessity forced to an extreme coincidence of individual and
class interests; their community is thus, to a greater extent than
past class associations, a community of individuals.[21]

Moreover—unlike past ruling classes—again due to its being
propertyless, the proletariat can only administer society in a
collective fashion, thus securing a collective administration of
society by the whole of society as soon as the whole of society
is reduced to the proletariat's state. In this way it can be seen
that when the proletariat, like any ruling class before it, asserts
its interest as the general interest in its hegemony over society,
it ultimately unveils the real general interest, that is, the process
of producing for society what it wants and needs.

What, though, will this proletarian state look like as it
emerges from capitalism? This, of course, will be dependent on
the specific circumstances of its emergence. In 1848, Marx saw
the following ten point program for a workers' state as "in the
most advanced countries ... pretty generally applicable":[22]

1. Abolition of property in land and application of all rents of land
   to public purposes.
2. A heavy progressive or graduated income tax.
3. Abolition of all right of inheritance.
4. Confiscation of the property of all emigrants and rebels.
5. Centralization of credit in the hands of the state, by means of
   a national bank with state capital and an exclusive monopoly.
6. Centralization of the means of communication and transport in
   the hands of the state.
7. Extension of factories and instruments of production owned by
   the state; the bringing into cultivation of waste lands, and the
   improvement of the soil generally in accordance with a common
   plan.

8. Equal liability of all to labour. Establishment of industrial armies, especially in agriculture.
9. Combination of agriculture with manufacturing industries; gradual abolition of the distinction between town and country, by a more equable distribution of the population over the country.
10. Free education for all children in public schools. Abolition of children's factory labour in its present form. Combination of education with industrial production, etc.

There are several features in this program that are worth noting. First, as Shlomo Avinieri has observed, the program is not so haphazard as it might at first appear to be.[23] It seems, in fact, to be designed to allow as "peaceful and orderly" a transition from capitalism to communism as possible. Industry, for one thing, is not even immediately to be nationalized when it is controlled by pliant capitalists who are neither emigrants nor rebels. How many of these in fact there are likely to be in any situation of social upheaval is, of course, difficult to say, and Avinieri perhaps makes too much of it in characterizing it as the program's "most amazing feature"; but still it is an amazing enough feature, considering both the aims of the workers' state and the usual stereotype of Marx and Marxists as intransigent revolutionaries who would like to turn the world upside down overnight. The combined features of abolition of inheritance and landed productive property, a truly progressive income tax and, especially, the centralization of credit in the hands of a socialist state should indeed render private ownership transitory, but it certainly is not a phenomenon that would wither immediately under them.

Second, the last clause in the seventh point in the program speaks directly to agricultural problems. This theme will be taken up again in the first volume of *Capital* where Marx argues that capitalist inroads in agriculture, though improving productivity, do so in an overall ecologically unsound manner, "all progress in increasing the fertility of the soil for a given time" under capitalism being in the long run "a progress towards ruining the lasting sources of that fertility."[24] In a somewhat rhetorical flourish he adds that capitalism develops both technology and the unification of social production "only by sapping the original sources of all wealth—the soil and the labourer." This unification as well as the development of technology will be carried on in a more rational manner by the revolutionary government in the *Manifesto* program in accordance with points five, six, seven, and nine. In fact, the entire program, as Marx himself summarizes it, can be seen as having as its purpose these two goals. For the primary aims of the new state must, according to him, be "by degrees ... to centralize all instruments of production in the hands of the state ... and to increase the total of productive forces as rapidly as possible."

"Communication" as the term is used in the sixth point, it should be finally noted, especially in these totalitarian latter days, most probably refers only to the mails and telegraph, not the press; Marx everywhere seems to be a staunch supporter of a free press as well as freedom of expression generally. Such methods as advocated in the ten-point program, nonetheless, he freely admits, most certainly *do* involve "despotic inroads on the rights of property and on the conditions of bourgeois production." The program, despite its moderation, could not possibly be accepted easily by the bourgeoisie; for the proletariat must of necessity "sweep away by force the old conditions of production." In doing so its measures will, moreover, seem both "economically insufficient and untenable" at first, as revolutionary measures always do. Soon, however, they will in fact "outstrip themselves" and "necessitate [even] further inroads upon the old social order." Such a course of events is "unavoidable as a means of entirely revolutionizing the mode of production."

One finds what may be an even earlier account of the first, transitional phases of communism in the *1844 Manuscripts* where Marx speaks of "crude communism," a form of "universal envy" which contains, as much as the capitalism from which it springs, the notion that "physical possession ... [is] the unique goal of life and existence."[25] This "crude communism" involves a barbarization of values and the worst kind of social leveling, including the desire "to eliminate talent ... by *force.*" Its paradigm is found in its attitude toward sexuality, the so-called "community of women." For "just as women are [in it] to pass from marriage to universal prostitution, so the whole world of wealth ... is to pass from the relation of exclusive marriage with the private owner to the relation of universal prostitution with the community." There are elements of the transition as later developed in Marx's thought in this version of communism. For example, in it the "role of *worker* is not abolished, but is extended to all men" while the transference of property to society still conceives of property along bourgeois lines, regarding the community as merely a "universal capitalist"; but it seems in context to be primarily an account of phases in the development of extant proletarian, communist ideology—or at most a projection with this as its basis—rather than speculation concerning a real program for a politically unified proletariat's assumption of power. Thus, it is hard to know how seriously to take its specifics. As to the notorious "community of women" it appears again clearly as paranoic bourgeois propaganda in the *Manifesto* four years later, in which Marx states that communism must entail the elimination of "prostitution, both public and private," i.e., the submission of women in bourgeois marriage, which serves as the community of women under capitalism.[26] At any rate, however we read the 1844 material, it does not—despite what some theorists, notably Avinieri, maintain—have anything but the most general features in common with Marx's later political commentary in the *Critique of the Gotha Program* or anywhere else.

The next place where we might be thought to find Marx commenting upon the transitional form of communism is in his observations on the 1871 Paris Commune in *The Civil War in France*. The Commune, of course, as we have already seen, was largely a mixed bag, a union of "the middling bourgeoisie and the petty middle class" shopkeepers and tradesmen with the working class; and Marx was, to say the least, never a wholehearted advocate of either the commune's establishment or the course it chose to take. Ten years after its founding, he was to describe it as incapable of fulfilling the minimal condition for a socialist seizure of power, namely, the ability to "take the necessary measures for intimidating the bulk of the bourgeoisie, which is the first *desideratum* in order that time for lasting action be gained," referring to it as "merely the rising of a city under exceptional conditions" and adding that "the majority of the Commune was in no way socialist, and could not be."[27] He thereupon declares that common sense would have dictated a compromise with its Versailles adversaries as being both its only realistic option as well as a move "useful to the whole mass of the people."

This latter comment perhaps sheds light on Marx's somewhat confusing attitude toward the Commune in his writings of 1871. Rather than a transitional form of communism proper it seems to be for him at best a possible form for the transition to communism. In the *Manifesto* he has said that the first step in the communist revolution must be for the proletariat "to win the battle of democracy." The Commune, had it been successful, would certainly have been a decisive step toward that goal. In the first place, both the Commune's democratic form and its plan to decentralize government in France, restoring "to the social body all the forces hitherto absorbed by the state parasite feeding upon, and clogging the free movement of, society," would have provided optimal conditions for the political development of the class struggle.[28] Though Marx might encourage the centralization of the bourgeois state in Germany as a prerequisite for further development, in France he clearly feels it has run its useful course and merely hinders the developing struggle.[29] The Commune, on the other hand, "affords the rational medium in which that class struggle can run through its different phases in the most rational and humane way."[30] Second, in the Commune, the working class provided the political leadership for its middling bourgeois and petit bourgeois allies, for the first time being "openly acknowledged [by the latter especially] as the only class capable of social initiative."[31] The government of the Commune was thus always in theory, though not nearly so clearly in practice, a workers' government. In Marx's own words it was "essentially" such, though certainly "the working class did not expect miracles from the Commune" and had, in the line already quoted earlier, "no ready-made utopias to introduce." The workers involved in the Commune in fact knew "that in order to work out their own emancipation and along with it that higher form to which present society is irrestibly tending by its own economic agencies" they would "have to pass through long struggles, through a series of historic processes, transforming circumstances and men." Still, as "essentially a working-class government," it was at least "the political form at last discovered under which to work out the economic emancipation of labor." This was its "true secret." It was thus for this reason that it posed such a threat to the Versailles government. For had it survived or even managed to wring extensive concessions from Versailles on reaching a settlement with it, the power and prestige of the proletariat would have been, in future political developments, immense.[32]

Theoretically a workers' government, the Commune did make some efforts toward socialism. The factories of emigrants were, in accordance with the advice of the *Manifesto,* seized and turned over to associations of workingmen; democratic measures of instant recall, which Marx obviously feels were of decided advantage to the working class, were furthermore introduced. Aside from these, however—and the latter is, of course, not explicitly and exclusively socialist anyway—only a handful of social legislation was enacted which was of definite advantage to the proletariat: the outlawing of night work for journeymen bakers, the banning of employers' fines, the recognition of the right of common-law wives (prevalent among the proletariat) to government militiamen's pensions, etc. Finally, in a spirit of proletarian internationalism the Commune accepted the right of foreign nationals to hold office, electing a German member of the International, Leo Fränckel, to a government seat.

Despite these measures and a good deal of communist rhetoric on the part of the representatives of the proletariat, it seems fair to say that we can perhaps discover more about transitional forms of communism from the limitations of the Commune from the proletarian viewpoint than in any real, positive efforts it made to impose proletarian class rule. Marx may have continued to view its form as *the* "form at last discovered" which would lead to the first phase of communism; though to understand him as doing so in some rigid fashion—measuring political progress against the Commune as prototype—would be to fail to recognize the flexibility of his politics; in fact, since he saw from the outset the Commune's inevitable failure, it is doubtful he is here speaking so literally; moreover, the attitude of the letter of ten years after reinforces this doubt.[33] At any rate, whatever the Commune's status for Marx, he never saw it as the first phase of communism itself.

The only reference to the initial phase of communism besides that of the *Manifesto* which is both straightforward *and* relatively extensive is in fact that found in the *Critique of the Gotha Program* which Marx wrote in response to the adoption of Lassallean principles by the newly unified German workers' party in 1875.[34] Here we find some rather detailed information on the possible economic structure of a late nineteenth-century socialist society. The "total social product" cannot be, he points out, as Lassalle would have it, simply redistributed among either the working class or society generally.[35] First of all, just as under capitalism a portion of profit is needed for reinvestment, so under communism a portion of the social product must be used "for replacement of the means of production used up" in production as well as "for expansion of production." This latter in the beginning phase of communism is especially important to Marx since, under nineteenth-century conditions—and indeed, taking a global view, in the twentieth century also—capitalism had come nowhere near the potential of providing a living level that could be reasonably seen as optimal for the mass of men; it was, in fact (as previously mentioned and as I shall elaborate upon it later), in the process of becoming a hindrance to further development of the productive forces;[36] socialism is seen by Marx as needed, among other reasons, to ensure that "all the springs of cooperative wealth flow more abundantly." A second reason that a simple redistribution of the social product is inadequate is seen in the need for a reserve "to provide against accidents, dislocations caused by natural calamities, etc." as well as "the general costs of administration not belonging to production," though this latter will be reduced under communism and continue to be so "in proportion as the new society develops," that is, as administration becomes increasingly the task of the associated producers themselves. It is interesting to note here that Marx feels, at least in the third volume of *Capital,* that external work discipline can apparently even in this first phase be eliminated, since workers are already—in much the same way as they are under piece work where work discipline is "practically superflous"—working for their own account.[37] Finally, deductions from the social product must be made for "those unable to work" and for those services such as schools, hospitals, etc. "intended for the common satisfaction of all."

Once these deductions have been made, the total social product can be divided; but in the first phase of communism, still imprinted with the mark of the capitalism from which it has emerged, the individual producers cannot yet see themselves as—for in fact they have not yet fully become—a society consisting of freely associated producers. What each is given then, after the above deductions, is compensation for "his individual quantum of labour" in the form of "a certificate from society that he has furnished such and such an amount of labour. . . . with this certificate he draws from the social stock of means of consumption as much as costs the same amount of labour." In this way, less deductions for the common funds, he then gets back exactly what he puts in. The measure of labor here used is the worker's portion of the "social working day," that is, the total number of hours of work in the day put in by the society as a whole. It is not altogether clear in what Marx says if this measure is further to be weighted according to the degree of skill necessary to his work or not.[38]

Such a system, Marx adds, is still based, of course, on the same principle as that which governs commodity exchange under capitalism, where, as we shall see, labor also provides the measure. This is one of the necessary limitations imposed by the circumstances of its birth. Though it has suppressed class differences—since "everyone is only a worker like everyone else" —its view of equality is still essentially bourgeois as "it tacitly recognizes unequal individual endowment and thus productive capacity as natural privileges." The right to receive back what one puts in is thus "a right of inequality, in its content, like every [other] right."

This latter addendum, though it is often taken by Marx's opponents as an avowal of antilibertarian sentiment, is, on examination of his further explanation, seen not to be. Rather he is pointing to the fact that rights of necessity apply equal standards to unequal cases, a method which he apparently feels can be superceded entirely by a society of fully socialized persons. Whether this is a reasonable expectation or not is difficult to say—it is indeed highly theoretical, being founded on a fairly

strict interpretation of the parallel between culture generally
and social relations. For on Marx's view, the free association of
producers in the "higher phase" of communism, involving a complete supercession of the notion of right with regard to social
wealth, must in its turn form the basis for the supercession of the
concept of "right" itself. It is in this society that the last traces
of exchange vanish and each member of society can, from a
a world grown more abundant under communist development,
take whatever he needs. Whatever change in legal structure
this radical social change ultimately entails, it is certainly safe
to say that with its advent the notion of "right" will undergo
a fundamental change.

Marx ends his discussion of the transitional phase of communism and the passage to the higher phase with the advice
to his readers that, since the productive conditions are the
determining factor for distribution anyway, it is "in general a
mistake to make a fuss about so-called *distribution* and put the
principal stress on it." For the presentation of socialism to dwell
on distribution in isolation from the mode of production is
to readopt the bourgeois economists' practice and retrogress.
The above account is a unique exception to this general policy,
called forth only in response to a discussion of distribution which
he did not begin.

In the *Critique of the Gotha Program* also Marx uses the now
famous and controversial phrase "dictatorship of the proletariat."
It is not the first time he has used the phrase—in fact, it is the
last instance of its use by him. There are seven other references
in all to it in his entire writings; three are in the 1850 *Class
Struggles in France;* two more the same year appear in an
agreement signed with the Blanquists in London exile and a
letter to the editor of the *Neue Deutsche Zeitung* concerning a
review of *Class Struggles;* a sixth is in a letter to Weydemeyer
in March, 1852; and the seventh is found in an article printed in
an Italian journal in January, 1873.[39] Lenin quotes this last in
his *State and Revolution* and makes quite extensive use of the
term in his political writings generally; it has also been used
extensively by apologists for the Soviet state—for example, by
Louis Althusser—who see in it a means of justifying the autocracy
of Stalin's rule as well as the high-handedness of the bureaucracy

that has developed under that rule. The notion of "dictatorship of the proletariat" as employed by Marx cannot, however, in any plausible way, be so read. As Hal Draper has shown in an exhaustive study of the context of its use, the phrase seems in practice to be synonymous with the more neutral-sounding "rule of the proletariat" found in the *Manifesto* references to the transitional workers' state as well as elsewhere in Marx's writings.[40] It appears around the years 1850–1852 and 1872–1875 and nowhere in between because only in these years, following unsuccessful revolutions in France, does Marx have extensive contact with the Blanquist refugees of these revolts. As the Blanquists held the view that a dictatorship of a relatively small elite was necessary in the beginning phases of the social revolution, both Marx and Engels were at pains to distinguish their views from those of these political allies as well as to influence them; hence, the currency of the usage "dictatorship of the proletariat," i.e., as opposed to the dictatorship of an elite.

Draper's further contention that Marx's espousal of the democracy of the Commune demonstrates that the proletarian class rule—or, if you will, dictatorship of the proletariat—must be democratic is, of course, mistaken, since, as we have seen, the Commune was for Marx never viewed as an instance of such rule. It is only Engels—whom he follows in presenting this argument—who identifies the Commune with the actual rule of the proletariat, *calling it* in fact "the dictatorship of the proletariat" in his 1891 preface to *The Civil War in France*. Again Draper's references to the call for a democratic republic in Germany which we find in the *Critique of the Gotha Program* are irrelevant, as Marx is here clearly talking only of a prerevolutionary phase, as with the Commune, where democracy can provide the final battleground for the class struggle.[41] Still, there is in fact strong internal evidence that the proletarian dictatorship can be democratic in form. When Marx, in his 1873 article, uses the phrase he compares it to the current social situation which he calls "dictatorship of the bourgeois class"—thus, as Draper rightly observes, "putting the accent on the social basis of power rather than on the political forms of the regime." For certainly the bourgeois dictatorship can be democratic. Since it also, of course, need not be, the question of the political form of the proletarian dictatorship or class rule is still open. However, when we note that Marx both expects the revolution to take place on a background of democracy and to bear the marks of its birth, we should expect it to contain more than mere traces of a democratic form.[42] Furthermore, among the proletarians themselves, it seems of the utmost importance that democracy prevail if the class is to develop into an association of individual producers; even initially, the collective control of property in the first phase of communism is difficult to conceive of in the absence of a class-wide democracy; this alone would seem to insure that the "dictatorship" was of a class rather than a Blanquist elite;[43] still, of course, this working class democracy need not, in fact in many areas most certainly cannot, extend beyond the class. Force and a certain despotism are inseparable from any revolutionary social change—in this sense, a class dictatorship would most certainly have to prevail. Just as the bourgeoisie, whatever the political form of its rule, does not let socialism emerge when it can stop it, so the proletarian government will necessarily suppress counterrevolution.

But perhaps we should speak further of the prerevolutionary background as well as of the revolutionary seizure of political power which emerges from it. To summarize, we may note that democracy is that form of the bourgeois state which allows for the greatest and most accelerated development of the class struggle. The power of the state, which always retards the struggle via its intervention, and is thus a direct hindrance to the proletariat once that class is well constituted, is minimized in the democratic form in that its actual initiatives more clearly approximate the resultant of the struggle than do other forms. Still more important, the democratic form allows organization to proceed most freely, and interferes least with the discussion and propagation of socialist and protosocialist ideas. For these reasons, in his above-mentioned comment on the Gotha Program, Marx says that "it is precisely in this last form of state of bourgeois society that the class struggle has to be fought out to a conclusion."[44] It was, moreover, such reasons among others that recommended the form of the Commune to him as well. Marx, in fact, throughout his career as socialist, tended to ally himself in general with all democratic movements. The observation about

"winning the battle of democracy" in the *Manifesto,* which I have
quoted above, may in fact refer only to the final imposition of
rule by an emerging proletarian majority as the middle classes
succumb and disappear with capitalist development and not to
any particular political form; but Marx was ever aware of the
need to foster bourgeois democracy in the interests of the
revolution.

Up until the time of the publication of the first volume of
Capital, the revolutionary transformation clearly is nonetheless
seen by him as being necessarily extraparliamentary;[45] force, he
tells us there, is the "midwife of every old society pregnant with
a new one" and an "economic power" in itself.[46] Still, we should
not, he adds several pages later, expect the proletarian revolution to be either as protracted or as violent as that which founded
capitalism.[47] For whereas in the capitalist revolution we observed the difficult "expropriation of the mass of the people by
a few usurpers," in the socialist "we have the expropriation of
a few usurpers by the mass of the people." The revolution will,
furthermore, be most humane in those nations where the working class has developed itself furthest politically at the time
when it occurs; it will in all probability also begin in these,
though it should prove contagious.[48]

By the early 1870s Marx seems to be of the opinion that it can
be—though not of necessity will be—so humane in certain countries as to preclude the need for force. Thus he told the 1872
Hague meeting of the International:[49]

We know that heed must be paid to the institutions, customs, and
traditions of the various countries, and we do not deny that there
are countries, such as America and England, and if I was familiar
with its institutions, I might include Holland, where the workers may
attain their goal by peaceful means.

By late 1880, in a letter to H. M. Hyndman, he expresses the view
that England's "unavoidable evolution" will turn into violent
revolution only if both the ruling class and the workers make a
blunder of things.[50] Before we jump to the conclusion that Marx
was in his last years well on his way to becoming the Willy
Brandt of the Victorian era, however, it should be noted that

less than a year and a half earlier he and Engels had attacked
the original reformists in the German Social Democratic Party
for claiming "that the workers are too uneducated to emancipate
themselves but must first be emancipated from the top down, by
the philanthropic big and petty bourgeois."[51] Marx's notion of
evolution in the English situation clearly does not abandon the
notion of class struggle; hence it can in no way capitulate to
reformism; it seems, rather, simply to mark off the English social
transformation as possibly peaceful and parliamentary in much
the same manner as his 1872 statement did. This former statement is immediately followed, it should furthermore be noted,
by the admonition that "we must also recognize the fact that in
most countries on the Continent the lever of our revolution must
be force." Marx's tactics remained always flexible and specific
to the situation. The advancement of the political struggle under
democratic conditions did, however, seem clearly to him to pave
the way for a minimum of force in transition, a goal which, as
we saw, he held from the beginning to be valuable—presumably
for tactical reasons as well as humane ones. It should likewise
not be forgotten, though, that as the recent example of Chile,
as well as several other instances in the past, have taught us,
taking power legally in no way precludes the need for force in
holding it. Marx seems clearly to have recognized this as late
as 1881 when he tells Anton Niewenhuis, the Dutch socialist,
in the above-cited letter of February 22 that the *sine qua non*
of a socialist seizure of power is the ability to secure time for
lasting action through intimidation of the mass of the bourgeoisie.
   Marx's view of both the seizure of power and the developments
which can lead to it is, as is indicated by the foregoing—as
well as by the first chapter—one of a political seizure with
political development as its prerequisite; this is as much the
case where the seizure is abrupt and dependent on somewhat
accidental disruptive circumstances (as it is in most revolutionary
situations) as where, as is possible in England, it blossoms more
slowly. A precise account of what Marx considers the exact
range of developments that can be considered political is therefore invaluable for clarifying his position. Happily, in an 1871
letter to Friedrich Bolte, an American member of the International, he provides just that.[52] The political movement of

the class has, he says, political power as its goal and "a previous organization of the working class developed up to a certain point" as its requirement. This latter, however, is "itself a result of its economic struggles." What distinguishes these from political struggles proper is their fragmentary nature. A strike in a particular factory or industry to force shorter hours is "a purely economic movement," unlike a movement to compel an eight-hour-day law which is political. In short, "every movement in which the working class as a *class* confronts the ruling classes and tries to defeat them by pressure from without is a political movement." Anything short of such a movement "which possesses general, socially coercive force" is not. Yet lesser actions can tend to lead to it, just as its first political successes lead the class on more boldly; they are thus to be encouraged. Constant agitation against capital's policies is the political training ground for the working class.

This emphasis in Marx's writings on politics and, especially, the political seizure of power, has led to an interesting criticism by the contemporary anarchist writer Murray Bookchin, who claims that there is an asymmetry between the bourgeois revolution and the proletarian revolution so conceived, insofar as "the bourgeoisie controlled economic life long before it took state power" whereas the proletariat never can.[53] There is an error, however, in such a criticism, I believe, in that the asymmetry in question is not so clearly present. Although complete dominance of the economy prior to the seizure of political power is, of course, impossible for the proletariat, developing as it does only as its bourgeois antagonist develops, in the course of the class struggle over the past fifty or so years, a reasonable case can be made for a view of the proletariat as singularly aggressive, as having put the bourgeoisie largely on the defensive, and, as being, in fact precisely in the process of conquering the economy politically for itself. It is ironic that, whereas the enemies of labor are in general fully aware and quite terrified of the economic and social power it has already obtained, the left for the most part regards it as largely powerless. This failure of observation can in part be explained by the already alluded-to misunderstanding of what rule by a ruling class in the Marxist sense entails; it is further fostered by an ambiguity in Marx's own presentation of the prospects for future struggle which we will turn to in Chapter 6; even more importantly, however, it seems to spring from the working class' refusal to embrace in a truly serious fashion any of the various ideologies which the left has dangled before it or to act upon them—especially in the current hub of capitalist society, the United States; since the proletariat has rather pushed its struggle in a direction more of its own choosing, its successes cannot be recognized as such by the left. The class struggle we are told has been "co-opted into capitalism";[54] one must therefore either ignore the proletariat in future practice or one must try to "reeducate" it; the former course is that of the new left and the leftist "irregulars" generally, the latter the way of the numerous Marxist sects.

Still, Bookchin's observation does point—albeit obliquely—to a possible general weakness in Marx's own political analysis in that, conservative as he sometimes was in his estimates of how long it would take for the workers' political self-development, he seems fairly clearly not to have anticipated anything like near economic hegemony as a prerequisite for political seizure. And yet, as I shall argue later, it seems to me increasingly clear that this may well be the case. Marx believed that the proletarian revolution would be far less protracted than the bourgeois; but it still has not reached fruition today, nearly a hundred years after his death.

CHAPTER 4

Methodology: Materialism and the Marxian Dialectic

THOUGH Engels has written at some length on materialism, Marx's own work contains very little which explicitly concerns the philosophy.[1] Of course, implicit in his entire work one can find a viewpoint that can be so described and any account of his materialist approach will need to be shown to be compatible with it; but if we want to discover the general framework, the number of sources we have at our disposal is scant. In this vacuum it is tempting to rely on Engels, as many writers (for example, Lenin) have, and treat the two authors as if they necessarily shared a theory. But, although we may find the Engels/Marx bifurcation excessive in some commentators on Marxism, it is at least highly problematic to assume full agreement.[2] Moreover, I believe that Marx in fact fails to deal systematically with the subject precisely because he, unlike Engels, has little interest in philosophy per se and has an interest in what they both call the materialist "viewpoint" only as a methodology for his work; we are thus ill advised in pursuing what was essentially a hobby of Engels too far in trying to gain an understanding of what Marx really has to say. In light of this, I shall in the following concentrate on the little we have available in Marx himself and only introduce Engels's observations in much the same way I would any other commentator on Marx. I shall, moreover, deal with materialism as Marx did—that is, as a methodology of his work and not as a world view or metaphysic.

I Marx on Classical Materialism

In his preface to *A Contribution to the Critique of Political Economy*, Marx tells us that, on his reexamination of Hegel's philosophy of law in the early 1840s, he discovered that not only is social consciousness not fully explained by reference to a "general development of the human mind" but that, on the contrary, it originates in "the material conditions of life." The economic structure forms a material base "on which arises a legal and political superstructure." This viewpoint, he further tells us, became "the guiding principle" of his studies.[3] Taken at its face value this can be read as the view that we are all the unwitting objects of impersonal economic forces, our consciousness a mere epiphenomenon which has no role other than as explicandum. Such a "vulgar economistic" interpretation of Marx's theory has been especially popular with his political enemies; for it is an easy view to criticize. However, it is not Marx's view and in fact rests on an understanding of the materialist outlook in social theory which Marx explicitly rejected.

Thus we find in the third of the *Theses on Feuerbach* that "the materialist doctrine [of previous materialist] social thinkers, that men are products of circumstances and upbringing, and that, therefore, changed men are products of other circumstances and changed upbringing, forgets that it is men that change circumstances."[4] Something is therefore missing for Marx in the above simple picture of the relation of the material world and the human mind. It is, he tells us, on looking back to the first thesis on Feuerbach, a conception of humans as active. The materialists conceived of reality only as an object to which we relate in a passive contemplative manner and hence failed to develop the subjective aspect of the situation, which is "human sensuous activity, practice." This failure in turn led the Utopian social thinkers—Marx mentions specifically Robert Owen—to assume that one needed only to change environmental conditions, thereby educating society, if one wanted to change society, the passive recipient of the lessons of external circumstances. But, notes Marx, the "educator himself needs educating." It will not do to divide society into two parts, as if the one, those who do the educating, is "superior to society" and immune from environmental influence, while the other is a mere pawn of environmental conditioning. We must instead understand "the coincidence of the changing of circumstances and of human activity" as "revolutionizing practice."

One cannot help but be reminded here of that modern utopian, B. F. Skinner who, working even today in the very tradition Marx here criticizes, perhaps opens himself to the same criticism which Marx made of his predecessors nearly a hundred years before. But, having noticed this, we are led immediately to the further question of how we are to conceive of this active side of the human situation in Marx. For surely the modern behaviorist representative of classical materialism would claim to account for it adequately through the introduction of "feedback" in the system—the world acts on men who in turn act on it in a manner which can be described via feedback loops.[5] Is this then the only innovation which Marx is actually urging? Or are we to see him, the thinker who has so often been cursed as a determinist, as advocating, on the contrary, a doctrine of free will—an unaccountable, subjective creative element? The description of the subjective, active side as "practice" and "human sensuous activity" sheds little light on this problem. However, his observation in the first thesis that "the *active* side, in contradistinction to materialism, was developed by idealism" might well do so. Introducing us to an approach to the problem which may well drive a wedge between the alternatives suggested above, it begins to reveal that which is distinctive in Marx's materialism. For Marx, though of course interested in characterizing himself as a materialist in order to show the affinity of his method to that of natural science, is, I suggest, as a dialectician, equally interested in distinguishing his approach from the idealism of the Hegelians.[6] In fact, in a sense, as we will see, to do the latter is to accomplish the former.

To begin to explore the murky depths of idealism in order to shed light on Marxian practice is ironic to say the least. Marx himself notes, after crediting the idealists with the development of the active side, that they developed it "only abstractly, since, of course, idealism does not know real, sensuous activity as such." Yet there seems to be no alternative. Marx never produced the essay which was to clarify and render "common sensical" his use of dialectics that he promised to Engels and Joseph Dietzgen, so we shall have to study his use of them against the idealist background from which it emerges. Let us then first turn to the subject of dialectics as developed by

Hegel, pausing from time to time along the way to note its positive influences on Marx's thought, and then pass from there to Marx's critique of it.

II *The Hegelian Dialectic*

Hegel is foremost a Rationalist. Though he recognizes contingency (*Zufälligkeit*) in nature as he conceives of it and apparently has no quarrel with—in fact even praises—empirical science as it functions in its own realm, philosophy for him, a more comprehensive endeavour than science, deals only with questions that can be answered *a priori,* mapping out a series of necessary connections between concepts. As such it is conceptual analysis for Hegel just as surely as it was for Plato or is for any contemporary philosophical analyst. Working in the tradition of Absolute Idealism which grew out of Kantian philosophy, he dismisses the earlier notion of Schelling that the Absolute, that is, the Totality or whole of reality conceived as Spirit, transcends our conceptual understanding. The Absolute is not an ineffable "I know not what" which needs to be treated mystically. The real is the rational; and the Absolute is reality. The task of philosophy then is to analyze our concepts as they express this reality. The analysis, however, has a form far different from that which we might unreflectively assume it to have. For the relationship between concepts with respect to the Absolute is a dialectical relationship and any deduction of one concept from another or others will proceed, not as a formal deduction would, but dialectically. Formal logic is in fact a kind of limiting case only; being formal, it deals only with the abstract form and not the content. As such, it treats conceptual relations only as "subjectivity," only insofar as they are forms of thought, not as they function with respect to reality, that is, the Absolute. A Rationalism which limits itself to formal relationships will never be able to comprehend the world in its totality; but a Rationalism that employs dialectical movement between concepts can.[7]

Thus, Hegel's Absolutism seems to have been the source of his development of dialectics. Reality or the Absolute must be understood as a unity of both the subjective and objective;

as such it is easily conceived in the manner of Aristotle's Prime Mover—pure Spirit thinking on itself, Absolute subject with itself as object. But whereas for Aristotle this Being exists independent of the world, exercising a telic pull on the beings in the world, for Hegel it *is* the world; the world is Absolute Spirit. The telos—if we are still justified in calling it that— is not an external pull but an expression of the necessary connections by which the world, conceived as Thought coming to think on itself, unfolds;[8] the process by which this unfolding occurs is the process of dialectical movement. Despite its having a teleological Absolutism as its origin, dialectics does not, however, seem to be inextricably bound to either notion in its functioning—a fact which Marx was quick to seize on in appropriating the method for his purposes; the telic pull is fully understood only via an understanding of the Absolute Spirit and the Absolute is fully understood only on its full unfolding. Hegel thus develops the logic of the unfolding without any essential reference to either.

At times this proves disconcerting as the "necessary" connections he elicits to move from concept to concept often seem curiously subjective and, at their worst, highly arbitrary; but it does allow the method to be set forth unencumbered by metaphysical commitment. As Marx puts it, "Hegel everywhere makes the Idea into the subject while the genuine, real subject . . . is turned into the predicate. The development, however, *always takes place on the side of the predicate.*"[9]

Though the dialectical method does not presuppose a Totality as Absolute Spirit, it does presuppose a whole—a whole, moreover, which is implicated in a consideration of any of its parts. No concept—*and,* since the real is the rational (conceptual), consequently, no thing—has reality in isolation from all others. All relations in the world, *when treated from a dialectical viewpoint,* are what have been traditionally called "internal relations."[10] Every concept is in fact united in the whole with its very opposite or opposites and, together with it or them, gives rise to yet another concept which is their unity in opposition. Thus, when dealing with dialectics in its most abstract form in his *Science of Logic,* Hegel points out that, beginning with the concept of the Absolute (reality) considered simply as Being without concrete determination, the mind passes readily to the "contradictory" concept of Nothingness, as Being without a determination is nothing.[11] The concept of the whole has now separated itself into two mutually exclusive, though dialectically related, concepts. The passage of consciousness from the one to the other gives rise to a "movement" which lays bare a still different concept, that of Becoming.

The term "contradiction" as used in dialectics is, of course, somewhat technical—not only because Hegel applies it derivatively to concepts per se rather than the statements or judgments in which they occur—but because it covers a wide variety of opposition, not merely explicit contradictions, as in the above example, but contraries as well—quantity and quality, essence and existence, master and slave, etc. all being viewed as dialectical "contradictions" by him. The concept of contradiction as employed in dialectics does not, moreover, imply a denial of the law of noncontradiction of formal logic, precisely because the contradictory elements do not remain in quiet coexistence as they would as presented by the static formal understanding; instead, they find their reconciliation in a movement which gives birth to a qualitatively distinct idea.

Consciousness is here alone the dynamic, and motion of consciousness the only way to understand such conceptual dynamics; but then consciousness is for Hegel ultimately not a mental product but reality itself. Thus, the term "movement" as used by Hegel may also be viewed as technical metaphor, provided we remember that—the conceptual, as noted, ultimately encompassing the concrete, both mental *and* physical—its use in Hegelan dialectical descriptions approaches the ordinary use of "movement" in a wide variety of cases. For Hegel, though notoriously abstruse, is surprisingly impatient with abstraction. He is, despite his rationalism, not a Plato who disdains the world of experience. Even the "motion" of the above illustration points to this—indeterminate Being passing to Nothingness because of its lack of determination. And when we examine his analyses in the *Philosophy of Right,* and, even more strikingly, in the *Phenomenology of Mind* this becomes abundantly clear.

Let me turn to this latter first. It is an early work and as

such its social theory is less tainted with the provincial nation-
alism to which Hegel at times succumbed after he had become
the official philosopher of the Prussian state. Written at a time
when Hegel championed both Napoleon's transformation of
the French Revolution into a state order and his consequent
exporting of its principles, which resulted in the destruction of
the vestiges of the feudal order in Europe, it approaches being
a social critique to perhaps the limit to which philosophy can
go. It was, moreover, for Marx the place where "Hegel's philosophy was born and that its secret is to be found."[12]

The *Phenomenology* is first of all phenomenology in the
usual contemporary sense of that term—that is, it is a general
descriptive study of the concept of mind or consciousness from
a viewpoint which holds at bay the "natural" attitude. Consciousness is in this study followed through a series of dialectical
supercessions which begins with consciousness of the world,
passes to an examination of self-consciousness, and from there
to the realms of Reason, Spirit, and Religion, finally ending
with Absolute knowledge as consciousness, which through its
dialectical movements, unfolds itself to itself as the world.
In the course of this demonstration, Hegel seems simultaneously
to develop various themes about philosophy per se—both moral
philosophy and epistemology—the history of ideas, and social
and psychological development; in doing so, he exhibits a
richness which has led to much confusion concerning his actual
intent; for our purposes here, however, we can consider all
and any of these illustrations of Hegelian dialectics at work
and ignore this question.

The first section of the *Phenomenology*, the analysis of consciousness of the external world, presents us with a critique
of conventional epistemology. In an analysis which anticipates
that of Wittgenstein and his followers nearly a century and
a half later, Hegel in a very short space disposes of the claims
of radical empiricists to base knowledge on sensation. Sense-
certainty—the indubitability of sense data—which might at first
"appear to be the richest kind of knowledge" and the most
concrete turns out, on examination, to be "the abstractest and
poorest kind of truth."[13] For the "Thises" and "this Heres"
that capture it lend themselves in almost no way to discursive

thought. Identity, reidentification, and description are all impossible at the level of sense-certainty; and so consciousness
passes on to simple perception, and finally to the sophisticated
"understanding" as set down in scientific law. But, having done
so, it finds satisfaction in this understanding only in that it
discovers itself in it; in the concepts of science, mind finds its
own constructs. "It is," says Hegel, "just for that reason that
there is so much satisfaction in [scientific] explanation."[14] Thus,
though scientific inquiry gives a richer truth than either sensation
or perception per se, its truth is incomplete. Consciousness now
becomes aware of itself for the first time as the truth, and
strives to know itself as it is, that is, it becomes self-conscious.
The ground of the passive understanding of the external world
turns out not to be that world itself, but an active consciousness.
This active consciousness becomes conscious of itself in turn
first in its active capacity of desire for things of the external
world; if the world is its world, it must show it to itself as
such by appropriating the external world and making it in
reality its own. Its self-understanding then further deepens as
it confronts an "object" which defies appropriation—another
self-consciousness; the social nature of consciousness has manifested itself.[15]

The supercession of epistemology herein carried out, though
accomplished in a decidedly idealistic framework, finds its
echo, it should be noted, in the second of Marx's *Theses on
Feuerbach*:

The question whether objective truth can be attributed to human
thinking is not a question of theory, but is a *practical* question. In
practice man must prove the truth, that is, the reality and power,
the this-sidedness of his thinking. The dispute over the reality or non-
reality of thinking which is isolated from practice is a purely
scholastic question.

Our knowledge of the world cannot be studied in isolation
from what we do and its results. Theoretical (epistemological)
studies of knowledge are necessarily barren. Those who hunt
for a theory of knowledge in Marx along traditional empiricist
or contemporary analytic lines will search in vain. Hegel, in

the process of developing the "subjective side" had already shown such attempts to be folly, and Marx accepts his verdict—not because the shadow of Hegel's Absolute Spirit has dimmed his vision, but because a purely passive understanding presents an incomplete, one-sided view of knowledge.

So we have in the *Phenomenology* moved from theoretical considerations of the relationship of consciousness and its object to man's needs as fulfilled in the world he inhabits and his social relations with other men—all by way of a phenomenological study of consciousness! But consciousness in this analysis has only begun to make itself concrete. With the treatment of the interrelation of two self-consciousnesses, the full power of dialectical analysis makes itself apparent. Whenever self-consciousness must confront another it necessarily seeks to "cancel this its other." For seeing itself in another "it has lost its own self" while not regarding "the other as essentially real" since it is, after all, itself which it sees.[16] Ultimately, full self-consciousness must accept the existence of the other self-consciousness as necessary to its own existence—that is, to frame this in the language of a more orthodox conceptual analysis, the concept of self-consciousness presupposes the concept of another. There is "a duplication of self-consciousness within its unity." But it is a duplication which necessarily involves another self-consciousness, its opposite. In concrete terms, that is, there are two self-consciousnesses unified in opposition to one another. And the first, most primitive expression of this opposition is an attempt at literal "cancellation" of one another, "a life and death struggle." The futility of such an attempt to undo the other—that is, oneself seen as an external other—soon, however, becomes apparent; for such a cancellation is not one which "preserves and maintains what is sublated" and hence does not survive its sublation. Life, self-consciousness learns, is essential to its existence. The resolution of this opposition must be attempted in a more sophisticated manner which preserves life.

The situation of the life and death struggle is reminiscent of the state of nature of Hobbes; the resolution of such a condition cannot be obtained by a social contract, however; the opposition is really present in the relation and cannot be denied.

It is the relationship of master and slave in which the opposition now presents itself in order that the sublated may survive its sublation and life be preserved. The master in this relationship thus appears as independent, as "the consciousness that exists *for itself*," while the bondsman is the sublated dependent who has existence only for the master. The master must be independent; it is through his independence that the bondsman is bondsman; the bondsman "takes up a negative attitude to things" in that he labors on them but does not himself appropriate them, as his labor belongs to the master, since it is the master's desire which controls his activity and the master who "gets the enjoyment" of its fruit; that is, "what is done by the bondsman is properly an action on the part of the master." The bondsman may shape the object, but it is the independent master's object which he shapes. There is, however, an irony in this which Hegel recognizes just as clearly as would Marx. The master, for all his independence of the bondsman, is in fact dependent. For the truth of his independence is found in the bondsman's recognition of his mastery and his consequent activity as bondsman. The concept of mastery presupposes that of bondage. Concretely, we find that, when the master appropriates the products of the bondsman as his property, he is really appropriating the bondsman's consciousness. The property which is the sign of the master's independence is really the embodied consciousness of the bondsman, the other and supposedly dependent one.

The bondsman's consciousness, for its part, is thus "the truth of the independent consciousness," that which it is in reality. This consciousness, though it may begin by seeing only the independent consciousness for itself in the master, through its fear of the master as expressed in its labor for the master, finally comes to itself. Since for it alone the objects the bondsman works on have independence—the master appropriating them only once they have been molded to his fancy—it alone, by forming them, can apprehend itself in and as the independence of the object. The bondman's activity is the "pure self-existence" of independent consciousness which through its accomplishments makes the consciousness external and permanent. Thus, says Hegel, "The consciousness that toils and serves accordingly attains by this means the direct apprehension of that independent being as its self." The bondsman in labor "becomes aware through this re-discovery of himself by himself, of having and being a 'mind of his own.'"

This analysis of the master/slave relationship is of extreme importance in understanding Marx's debt to Hegel. It will, as we will see in the next chapter, play a vital role in Marx's early writings on the alienation of labor. It also reiterates the claim referred to above which he shares with Hegel that knowledge is not to be thought of as something passive; for Hegel the claim may still, of course, be seen as branded with the mark of his idealism, since the objectivization of the self will eventually be swallowed up in Absolute Consciousness; nonetheless, the analysis itself seems to presuppose this outcome, if at all, only in its treatment of the dialectical movement as that of consciousness coming to self-consciousness. For our purpose here, however, by far the most important outcome of a study of the analysis lies in its handling of the concept of consciousness as it makes itself, both subjectively and objectively, concrete. Consciousness is not for Hegel, nor for Marx who follows him in this, having an idea in one's mind (or head). The bondsman to know himself in his works need not come to an explicit recognition which he can express in a judgment to the effect that he finds that the work embodies himself. The link between his activity and consciousness is far more intimate than that; his activity is consciousness embodying itself in his works.

From this we can begin to understand Marx's critique of classical materialism in the first thesis on Feuerbach more fully. To conceive of the conscious side of our relationship to the world as contemplative only is to fail to understand the active nature of consciousness—that consciousness is not a facsimile of the external world imprinted on the mind, but what we do as aware, purposive beings. To be conscious of one's class position, that is, to be class conscious, is not to hold views of oneself as a worker, bourgeois, farmer, etc., but to act in a manner which expresses one's social position. Politically, failure to understand this leads to the use of Marxist theory as an ideology, as if it were an evangelical religion passing on the "word" to the previously unenlightened; the progress of the struggle be-

tween capital and labor is from this mistaken viewpoint to
be judged by the number of converts to socialism so far
obtained or perhaps even by the number of converts to "Marxist"
socialism or to the particular variety of "Marxist" socialism
that the sect to which one belongs advocates. Thus,
Paul Sweezy has recently advised radicals that it is the task
of the left to educate the working class to socialism.[17] Over a
hundred years have passed and yet much of the left seems no
more aware than Robert Owen that "the educator himself
needs educating."

Returning to Hegel's *Phenomenology,* we find that for both
master and slave, interrelated as they are, a fully independent
self-consciousness is impossible; the slave, though he finds a
"mind of his own" in his labor, can exercise it only in stubborn-
ness; true freedom is antithetical to the conditions of slavery
for both master and slave. Thus are born attempts, futile though
they may be, to transcend the condition and achieve a free
and independent self-consciousness. The first is a retreat to
an inwardness which "has been called *Stoicism,* in so far as it
has appeared as a phenomenon conscious of itself in the course
of the history of man's spirit." This inwardness proving too
barren, consciousness tries to take cognizance of the external
world without taking it seriously through the adoption of the
attitude of *skepticism.* The world, however, will not disappear;
true freedom is impossible without dealing with the world. A
third attempt, the arising of the *Unhappy Consciousness* of the
"Alienated Soul" as exemplified in the Catholicism of the Middle
Ages, fares little better in that the opposition between two
selves which resulted in the unsatisfactoriness of the relation
of master and slave here appears in the relationship between
God and man. Yet such consciousness does set the stage for
the idea of Reason—that is, "the certainty that consciousness is,
in its particularity, inherently and essentially absolute, or is
all reality." The Otherness which the individual self-consciousness cannot absorb will be reintegrated into consciousness
through the dialectical development of this viewpoint of Reason
to which the dialectical developments of consciousness becoming aware of a natural and social world have painfully given
birth.

At first this Reason can only explicitly reveal itself in the empty form of philosophical Idealism—that is, the Idealism of Hegel's predecessors. It is implicitly able to develop, however, in the practical activities of social life; the dialectical movements of earlier phases of Hegel's *Phenomenology* are herein repeated in a more developed form. Reason in social development at the outset "is aware of itself merely as 'an individual' and must, being such, demand and bring forth its reality in an 'other.'"[18] It thereafter develops awareness of itself as "universal reason," however, and finally sees itself as the "Social Order" or "Ethical World," the "simple ultimate spiritual reality" as expressed in the unity of individuals living under one law and culture. In the course of this development from individual to universal, it moves from an individualistic and hedonistic pursuit of pleasure, which quickly runs afoul of the Other, through a sentimental Romanticism, which in its frustration is superceded by fanaticism, to an empty chivalry which fails to engage the world; it can only then come to grips with the world, understanding it as itself molded through its actions; but it still fails to understand social unity, since its interest in its actions as personal comprise their sole value for it. This individualism of competence is in turn superceded by Reason as moral legislator, molding individuals into a unified community through the establishment of moral laws, while in the meantime providing a constant critique of the laws which it has set down. The interactions of bourgeois economic life, what Hegel was later to call "Civil Society," are brought under the control of ethics here.

Reason becomes Spirit, Hegel then tells us, when it "is *consciously* aware of itself as its own world." At first ethical life is unreflective, rooted in family relationships; it becomes reflective, however, as Spirit moves into a phase of "self-estranged" cultural life. This cultural phase is exemplified in the development of modern society; social and economic units centralize and become more complex as consciousness knows the world more clearly to be its world to mold; reason operates critically in an effort to realize what it knows to be its own true nature in the world—that is, that consciousness is the world; the criticism is at times ruthless, periods of enlightenment with their critique of religion and the social order culminating in such events as the Terror of the French Revolution. This "self-destructive" phase proving fruitless, Spirit then leaves the political arena and turns back to morality, more fully self-conscious, however, than before; it is then superceded by religion, which in its turn gives way to Absolute Knowledge, the rationalized equivalent of religion which is the culmination of philosophical inquiry.

In these last sections of the *Phenomenology* the social and political disappear as Hegel becomes absorbed with pure thought. Fourteen years later, however, he again investigated social theory in his *Outline of the Philosophy of Right*.[19] The philosophy of right is for Hegel an investigation of "Objective Spirit," the concept of Spirit as it objectifies itself, making the world its world; the dialectical development of this concept moves us from the concept of right formally considered to morality as subjective to morality as expressed in social custom. Beginning with the concept of the free individual, Hegel finds that the freedom herein contained discovers itself in the appropriation of the external world; hence the notion of freedom is seen by him as entailing that of property. Property in its turn only reaches its full development with the introduction of the idea of a contract in which any number of individuals sort out and alter their property relations. These relations, it should be noted, are for Hegel between persons and concern things, namely, the things one appropriates; though one can sell one's labor, one cannot sell oneself or another; the concept of property examined here is clearly that of the bourgeois age. Property in its full sense as embodied in contract presupposes the possibility of violation of contract, moreover, and hence the introduction of the concept of wrong and that of punishment; crime and punishment are thus rooted in the institution of private property, a fact which Hegel himself explicitly notes.[20] Punishment is not seen here as a mere pragmatic device to insure the honoring of contracts; in it the *rational* will of the offender must necessarily acquiesce. The offender, however, is not necessarily rational and insofar as he is not the punishment seems merely an external sanction to him. In internalizing this sanction, thus making the individual will conform to the rational, namely, that of Spirit which recognizes itself as universal, we move to a personal moral viewpoint.

This somewhat Kantian and typically Protestant treatment of ethics is, however, made concrete only through its supercession by social ethics (*Sittlich Keit*) which by now, for an older, more firmly established and conservative Hegel, has come to occupy a higher level in dialectical progress than it did in the *Phenomenology*. Social ethics is, as previously, the expression of simple, unified reality, what Hegel now calls the "ethical substance." This substance unfolds itself in the family, civil society, and the state, one superceding the other, not in any temporal sense, of course, but as the full working out and coming to fruition, that is, self-consciousness, of the ethical substance. Thus the family, expressing itself in a familial love which unites and solidifies family property, gives way to a more complex form as its children are seen necessarily to reach maturity and form separate families of their own. This form is civil society, the world of the classical political economists. In it we find a group of self-interested individuals united in an economic system which is to their mutual advantage. This system, moreover, presupposes a social division of labor, corporate organization, and an administration of law. Hegel, in line with the somewhat backward development of the Germany of his day, terms the units of this broad division of labor "estates" rather than classes and paints a picture of the corporation as something partaking of both the form of bourgeois enterprises and the medieval guilds; the administration of the law is the work of the police. But this civil society is in turn seen to glean its unity only through the legally constituted state. The state thus supercedes civil society; in it the ethical substance reaches its goal. States do, of course, interact in world history, but this calls forth no higher synthesis, no world federation; international relations, including war, simply serve to develop states in the service of Spirit. The development of history is Spirit working out its course in the world.

III   *Dialectics in the Works of Marx*

We have seen in the above that dialectics as employed by Hegel is wedded to a philosophical, that is, a conceptual analysis even in those developmental accounts which appear most concrete. As such, the analysis cannot go beyond the concepts which form its subject matter; these being social products, it must, for all its insights, stay within the limits of the society from which it arises. Although by treating concepts dynamically it can, unlike past conceptual analyses, grasp the history and development of the concepts it analyzes and, derivatively, that of the social institutions they represent, it cannot go beyond them and point to future change. Hegel himself becomes explicit concerning this in his conservative later years when he notes and willingly accepts in the preface to the *Philosophy of Right* that "philosophy arrives always too late" to influence what the world ought to be. Though it can extract the current social ideal from the concepts it analyzes, "even the Platonic Republic ... has essentially taken up nothing but the nature of Greek ethics"; as his now famous line has it, "The owl of Minerva spreads its wings only at dusk."[21] Philosophy, he and Marx agree, can only understand the world; it cannot change it. Even when the concepts which are its staple are treated dynamically, they cannot extend their motions beyond themselves. At their worst, in Hegel's later work, these motions do not even encompass real temporal developments. The series of supercessions which we have traced in our account of the *Philosophy of Right* can, observes Marx, leave quite intact "in *actuality* private right, morality, the family, civil society, the state" in the very forms in which the philosopher finds them. The supercession of philosophical dialectics is "in thought, which leaves its object in existence in the real world" though it "believes itself to have really overcome it."[22]

Hegel has for Marx nevertheless accomplished much in the earlier *Phenomenology* in that he "grasps the self-creation of man as a process ... and that he, therefore, grasps the nature of *labour*, and conceives objective man (true, because real man) as the result of his *own labour*."[23] But he cannot develop these findings in that labor for him is "abstract mental labor," that is, the concept of labor, just as appropriation is only "an appropriation which occurs in *consciousness*, in *pure thought*, that is, in abstraction" from objects "as *thoughts* and as *movements of thought*."[24] Though, as noted above, Hegel anticipates Marx in his treatment of consciousness, and insofar as he does, has grasped the nature of labor from Marx's point of view, ultimately still for him "the true form of mind is thinking mind." The slave may know himself through his action in his works but the philosopher knows the relationship between the concept of slavery and that of the products produced therein; and the activity of the philosopher, philosophy, is for Hegel the paradigm and epitome of human activity, "my true human existence" for him being, as Marx puts it, "my existence in *philosophy.*"[25] Thus, after several hundred pages which approach being a concrete social analysis, the *Phenomenology* ends in the contemplative "absolute knowledge" of philosophy at its zenith. This results, as Marx notes, from the fact that "objectivity as such" is offensive to Hegelian (idealist) consciousness.

But, to attribute this movement merely to Hegel's idealism, is to miss the point; Hegel establishes himself as an idealist only by raising philosophy—the coming to self-knowledge of consciousness—to the heights which he does. Philosophy does not know the object per se; it knows only the concept of the object. Thus, when philosophy begins to pose as reality itself under the rubrics Consciousness, Reason, and Absolute Spirit, the concept is mistakenly taken for the object. Giving up the pose does not, however, set things straight in itself; so long as we are limited to philosophy, we are subject to its limitations. The Young Hegelians fared little better than Hegel himself in developing the insights inherent in Hegel, despite their substitution of Man for Absolute Spirit.

Marx, as we saw at the beginning of the chapter, though praising idealism for its development of the "active side" of human reality, criticized the idealist development as abstract. We now see the full significance of his critique. The materialist approach, that is, the methods and viewpoint of empirical science, must replace the mere philosophical approach of the idealists; once this is done—when dialectics is incorporated into a scientific methodology—the active side will be comprehended for what it is, not abstractly, but empirically, sensuously, as "human sensuous activity" in the world. Exactly what happens to dialectics when it becomes incorporated into a scientific methodology still, however, remains to be examined. Science

per se was left by Hegel at what was for him the incomplete
level of "understanding," a form into which content is squeezed
in a merely "external fashion."[26] The question is: What does a
science look like which has substituted the internal relations of
dialectical analysis for these external forms of understanding?

A full answer to this question can best be given by actually
looking at such a science, which is the primary task of this book;
but a general account of dialectics in Marx's social theory is both
possible within limits and desirable, insofar as it provides a basis
for understanding its use in the particular. This is not to say that
dialectics in Marx's work is especially obscure;[27] Marx seems
in practice really to *have* reduced Hegel's mysteries to a piece
of common sense; but the method is nonetheless quite distinct
from that employed in the orthodox—what Marxists call "the
bourgeois"—social sciences, just as much as it is from that of
Hegel's social theory. For this reason, a reflective understanding
of dialectics in Marx is of value in comprehending him and his
view of social life. Let me then begin this reflection by pointing
to the differences between the Marxian scientific and the Hegelian
philosophical dialectic.

In what has become a famous quotation, Marx says that in
Hegel the dialectic "is standing on its head" and "must be turned
right side up again, if you would discover the rational kernel
within the mystical shell."[28] For Hegel, he has just previously told
us, "the life process of the human brain . . . under the name of
'the Idea'" becomes "an independent subject . . . the demiurgos
of the real world, and the real world is only the external,
phenomenal form of 'the Idea.'" This appears to be a direct
reference to what he has earlier, following Feuerbach, described
in several places as an inverted relation of subject and predicate
in Hegel.[29] "Real man and real nature become" in the work of
Hegel "mere predicates," while consciousness posing as Absolute,
"unreal man and unreal nature," is the subject of dialectical
movement. Moreover, as previously noted, the mere removal of
the Absolute from the dialectic is not in itself enough; consciousness posing as Man in the Young Hegelians is as much
a reversal as Hegel's own. In Hegel's Rationalism we see an extreme instance of man's taking his thoughts to be "spirits existing outside nature and man."[30] But the taint of it is still present

in all philosophizing. It is necessary to replace consciousness as either God (Absolute Spirit) *or* Man with "real man and real nature" in dialectical interaction.

To do this is to adopt what Marx calls "naturalism," the natural attitude, an attitude which he in his early writings contrasts with both idealism and classical materialism.[31] On this view man is a natural being, that is, an objective being inhabiting a world of objective being. As "an *embodied,* living, real sentient, objective being with natural powers" he must have "*real, sensuous objects* as the objects of his being"; he can in fact "only express his being in real, sensuous objects." Feuerbach, whose work greatly influenced Marx in the adoption of this attitude—being the first to set right Hegel's subject/predicate inversion—nonetheless stopped short of it in that he did "not conceive human activity itself as objective activity," but regarded the purely subjective "theoretical attitude as the only genuinely human attitude."[32] By doing so, it became impossible for him to study humanity scientifically. The full power of the idealist dialectic made scientific could not be used.

The subject matter with which the scientific dialectician deals, write Marx and Engels in the coauthored *German Ideology,* is "real individuals, their activity and the material conditions under which they live, both those which they find already existing and those produced by their activity."[33] As such, it allows any assertions made about it to "be verified in a purely empirical way." The "necessity" of the Hegelian "logical" dialectic is thus no longer operative; the only necessity we can expect to find in dialectical explanations is the physical necessity of empirical law. Far from being necessary in the strict logical sense that Hegel envisioned, the Marxist dialectic, as we already saw in the second chapter, at times even underdetermines the situation; this, as will be made clear, is due both to its inherent nature as empirical and to the fact that it allows for the intervention in dialectical processes of largely accidental influences. Moreover, though human purposiveness enters in as an element in the dialectical process—as objective as any other element—there is no purpose or reason in the process per se. Whatever teleology may still linger on in Hegelian discussions is in a scientific dialectical account banished once and for all. We simply have a social world scientifically understood; purpose enters into the picture only in terms of application of this understanding. By moving from a philosophical to a scientific viewpoint we open up the possibility of changing as well as understanding the world.

What remains from the Hegelian dialectic, in addition to the particular features we have already noted in our discussion of Hegel, are the following general features: (1) a holistic theory with its attendant view of relations as internal; the dialectical moments in Marx's theory (whether social classes per se or more complex developments of social relations) are just as clearly as Hegel's only fully characterized in the context of the whole; as dialectical moments they can only coexist and have no real significance in isolation. To cite the simplest possible example of this, capitalists and wage workers have existence only in relation to one another within the system of capitalism; outside it and in themselves these social categories have no meaning because they exist *as* social categories only together in the relation called capitalism; in the absence of workers there could be no capitalists, but likewise, in the absence of capitalists, we could not identify any laborers as wage workers. Furthermore, these dialectical moments are, as dialectical moments, (2) moments in mutual "contradiction"; that is to say, they coexist only in antagonistic interaction. This interaction will, moreover, (3) undergo intensification—in the naturalistic, scientific dialectic a process which can only occur in time—until (4) a supercession of the original moments occurs in the form of a qualitatively different phenomenon which provides a resolution of the original antagonism, though it, of course, may give birth to a new dialectical antagonism in its turn.

Such a structure renders the range and nature of predictivity far different in dialectical science than it is in the mechanistic sciences which originally recommended the scientific method to both Marx and his classical materialist predecessors. A dialectical account can make only two exact predictions—those given in numbers (3) and (4) above, that the interaction of the dialectical moments will intensify over time and that they will eventually be superceded; at some reasonable interval $t + 1$ we should always be able to find a more intensified situation than was ob-

served at time t until which time a revolutionary (or degen-
erative) break occurs. The nature of these intensifying antagonisms may be extremely complex, as we saw in the second chapter,
though, on Marx's view, they will tend to simplify as society
divides progressively into the "two great hostile camps" of
bourgeoisie and proletariat.[34] Still, even as this comes to pass,
with the ascendancy of the bourgeois era, the precise form which
the intensification takes or will be likely to take must be left
to a concrete analysis of present conditions and the relatively
short-range possibilities which they present. Dialectical analysis
at its best, when skillfully employed, can lay out the full range
of possibilities—as Marx does in part, for example, in his discussions in *Capital* of the various tendencies within the capitalist
system—but it cannot set out which one will be chosen nor when
it will be in the course of dialectical development;[35] after the
fact explanation is always open to dialectics, but the course of
the antagonistic development is underdetermined in its details.

This is necessarily the case, that is, it is in the nature of
dialectical explanation, as the action of each dialectical moment
is dependent on the action of its opposite moment to which it is
a response; and within dialectics one cannot set out straightforward causal generalizations to trace this development; if
one could, then it would be possible in fact to replace the
dialectical analysis with a mechanistic one. For the same reason,
one cannot determine the precise time at which the intensification will lead to a qualitatively different supercession nor can
one determine the exact, detailed nature of the newly emergent
phenomenon. This latter follows from the fact that a dialectical
theory, unlike mechanistic accounts, does not simply deal with
motion, that is, quantitative change in a fixed quality, but with
actual qualitative change, thus rendering it impossible to
measure fully the change. Finally, since one cannot isolate
dialectical moments from one another, one cannot verify claims
concerning the tendencies of one moment in isolation from its
antagonists.[36]

The underdeterminations thus inherent in any dialectical
science, combined with those introduced through the medium
of historical accident, make Marxist theory extremely inefficient
in comparison to the best mechanistic theories with respect to

prediction.[37] This, however, would not necessarily provide a problem for Marx in that he seems not to locate the essence of scientific power in predictive power per se but in practice, the ability to make one's actions bring about an intended result. This after all is where science had proven itself and won recognition socially, namely, in the realm of practical application. Of course, the two, successful practice and predictive power, are directly proportional in the case of a natural science; the accuracy of detailed information which Newtonian mechanics provides can, for example, be nothing but helpful in the construction or repair of a steam engine. But when we deal with social theory this is no longer true. A fully deterministic social theory—*were* such a theory possible—could not aid social practice at all; it would be, as it were, totally removed from practice; one would merely have the luxury of passively watching society, as a natural process, run its course. Provided then that, within its range of prediction, Marxist theory is accurate, its limitations on this count present no absolute limitation on its scientific worth; one might desire more precision than the theory can provide for political practice; for, though the above claim concerning full determination holds, this in no way entails that predictive power is irrelevant in scientific social theory viewed from the "practical" point of view. Still, if social theory needs to use the methodology of dialectics, the increase of precision possible is, as we have seen, severely limited; whatever one's final decision on Marx's social theory itself, it must be admitted that he is a skillful dialectician who appears to be able to extract the ultimate power possible from the method, especially in *Capital* where the full power of the Marxist dialectic is most clearly revealed.

Thus, as against what Marcuse, Georg Lukács, Antonio Gramsci, and their followers believe, we see that we do not need to burden Marx with the inheritance of "the transcendent point of view of the philosophical critique" in order to keep him from falling victim to a Comtean positivistic variety of naturalism.[38] The social world on the positivist view is strictly analogous to the natural world in that "social movement is necessarily subject to invariant physical laws, instead of being governed by some kind of will."[39] Starting from this dichotomy of natural social process and human volition, positivism can then very quickly proceed to the recommendation of a "wise resignation" of the will in the face of these inexorable physical laws, a philosophy which Comte himself rather shamelessly touted as being invaluable in maintaining the public order. This naturalism suffers, it can be seen, from the very defect which Marx found in classical materialism—the subjective is in it excluded from the natural process rather than being seen as an objective, natural part of it; it is, it in fact seems fair to say, this very materialism responding to the needs of a mature bourgeoisie which no longer has need to encourage a revolutionary spirit.[40] Once one moves beyond such a materialism, incorporating the subjective aspect in the natural viewpoint, the subject as passive and noncritical is seen as an illusion; moreover, the adaptation of dialectics to this natural viewpoint banishes forever the possibility of any passage to positivism. The Marxian attitude does not cease to be critical because it ceases to be transcendent; for Marx the movement to naturalism removes criticism from the transcendent nether world of thought and places theory in the service of practice. The necessary underdetermination of a dialectical methodology guarantees the possibility of this critical edge.

This, however, still leaves open the question of whether a dialectical methodology is the only adequate or, at the very least, the best methodology with which to pursue the study of man as an "objective being," since the adoption of the Marxian natural attitude in no clear way seems to entail the adoption of dialectics. If, moreover, dialectics *is* the most adequate methodology possible, then it would follow that good social theories necessarily underdetermine their data, a curious fact, if it is a fact, which itself seems to call for an explanation. For Marx, of course, these questions never as such arose. He found dialectical theory in its idealist form as grasping, albeit abstractly, the subjective side of things and moved from this discovery to a more concrete formulation via adoption of naturalism—that is, Marx was already committed to a dialectical analysis at the time he moved to a naturalistic viewpoint. Once the dialectic is naturalized the wedge is necessarily left open for "practical-critical activity" and a theory which can be used for political action is readily at hand. The first question, that is to say, was for

Marx himself answered in practice itself, and clearly answered in the affirmative as he continued to make extensive use of a dialectical analysis in all his works. The second—since underdetermination is for Marx necessary to any adequate social theory—seems never to have occurred to him as a real question.

For us, though, it harks back to the questions with which we began our discussion of dialectics: Is the underdetermination to be seen as an expression of human agency in the sense of an inherent freedom in human action? Surely this is a possibility, and an affirmative answer to the question would seem to lay the basis for a demystified version of the Marcusean interpretation of Marxism as the struggle of "free rationality" with necessity.[41] I do not, however, see that we are obliged to answer this question in the affirmative in that the inability of a social theory to provide a full explanation of human activity does not in any way entail that supplementary theories are unavailable which can fill this gap. It is, of course, true that such theories, if they were to render Marxism *fully* deterministic, would leave no room for the critical edge of practice; but it is also true that, given that they are merely supplementary and hence operative only *within* the general dialectical framework of Marxist theory, they could not do so.[42] For, since a dialectical moment arises only in response to its opposite, the initial conditions under which the supplementary theories would be functioning would constantly change. We can also see therefore that this necessary underdetermination of dialectics clearly indicates that Marxist theory is not equivalent to a fully deterministic behaviorism with feedback, the alternative interpretation with which we began. Feedback incorporated into a behavioristic or other type of mechanistic social theory results in general in the Marxian methodological viewpoint *sans dialectic*. Moreover, it can in no way, as can a dialectical theory, account for truly qualitative as well as quantitative change.

We have in the above discussion nowhere addressed the question of whether dialectical methodology is inherently a methodology of *social* science alone.[43] Without embarking on a philosophical discussion of Engels's *Anti-Duhring* and *Dialectics of Nature*, a discussion which I at the outset promised to avoid as being—for our purposes—unrewarding, I should before closing comment upon this, at least insofar as it bears on the under-standing of dialectics as a scientific method. Dialectics cer-tainly seems to involve goal-directed activity of necessity, dialectical opposition being—even when, as in *Capital,* couched in the reified language of the bourgeois world—inherently an opposition of purposes. If we therefore reject functionalism in the biological sciences, it would seem that dialectical explanation should be limited to the behavior of men. The purposeful human behavior involved need not, of course, be individual nor need the purposes be, as we have seen, explicit in anyone save the dialectician's mind; yet they must nonetheless be intimately bound up with conscious, human activity. Any extension of dialectics into other areas of experience would seem to involve a certain metaphorical use of language and some degree of anthropomorphism, an approach which modern science, for better or worse, has usually shunned throughout its five-hundred-year history.[44]

Finally, we should not leave the subject of scientific dialectics without some general comments on the relationship between Marxian science and the ideological apparatus of class struggle.[45] Insofar as Marx's theory is a science *for* the proletariat, one might be inclined to ask whether it does not fail to be a true science, in that it would seem to be inextricably entangled in the ideology of this class. On the other hand, insofar as it is not so entangled, could it not prove useful to any class and hence not be a science for the workers? The answer to these questions is, I believe, that, as a science, Marxist theory is, within limits, a useful tool for the bourgeoisie as well as the proletariat. J. M. Keynes himself might not have used Marx in his work; but as Joan Robinson has very perceptively put it, it "would have saved him a lot of trouble" if he had. There is no question but that liberal reformism can most certainly benefit from Marx's understanding of the capitalist world. Severe limitations on this general usefulness are, however, found in the long range untenability of capitalism on the Marxist view. It is perhaps no accident that Lord Keynes, on being questioned on the long run implications of his measures to save capitalism, was forced to answer that in the long run we will all be dead.

IV *Materialism and Naturalism in Marx's Work*

In the above I have treated Marx's materialistic methodology as identical with his adoption of a scientific (naturalistic) attitude in the study of society, and *in practice,* I believe, this identification holds. There are, however, several passages where Marx speaks of his materialistic approach in a manner which, *prima facie* at least, may make it seem to involve more than the mere adoption of a scientific outlook. Thus, in a passage from *The German Ideology* he speaks of the "fundamental form" of human social activity as "material, from which depend all other forms—mental, political, religious, etc."[46] Likewise, in a note in the first volume of *Capital,* he stresses the necessity of studying the history of technology on the ground that "technology discloses man's mode of dealing with Nature, the process of production by which he sustains his life, and thereby also lays bare the mode of formation of his social relations, and of the mental conceptions that flow from them."[47] A similar passage can be found already present in the early *Economic and Philosophical Manuscripts of 1844* as well.[48] Moreover, in these manuscripts we find Marx speaking of "religion, the family, the state, law, morality, science, art, etc." as "particular forms of production" subordinate to material production.[49] The passage regarding the primacy of material life which is found in the preface to *A Contribution to the Critique of Political Economy* I have already cited in the second section of the present chapter.

Are we compelled then ultimately—at least on the basis of such passages—to see Marx as excluding ideological factors from his explanations` as part and parcel of his materialist methodology? We have already seen that the still stronger thesis that men are the passive pawns of material forces is *not* what Marx is maintaining in his materialism, that in fact it is this thesis which he regards as the chief defect in previous materialisms; but to deny this stronger thesis in no way precludes him from adopting the weaker one that would deny causal efficacy to men's *ideologies;* human activities are certainly not limited to the expression of ideas. On the other hand, the adoption of the natural attitude in itself would in no way force this latter thesis upon him. When a naturalistic position is adopted, the ideas of an era become—as expressed in verbal acts—events or phenomena, that is, pieces of human behavior, on a par with any other behavior; the adoption of the position only insures that they will not be accepted at face value as explanations *in themselves* of social dynamics; but, like any other phenomena, causal efficacy is open to them still. Why then does Marx in these passages seem to deny them such efficacy?

If we look at Marx's social theory itself, we find the answer to this question without much difficulty: that the causal efficacy of ideas is—at least with regard to the most general features of social movement—negligible is a part of the actual hypothesis of Marx's social thought; it is an integral component of the theory. As such, this aspect of his materialism is not a general methodological presupposition but a straightforward aspect of his science, while materialism as methodology is limited to his above-described fully naturalistic, scientific approach to the study of society. Marx himself, I suggest, never clearly and explicitly distinguished these two (distinguishable) aspects of his materialism; nor in his work did it matter in any practical way that he did not. Still, the conflation of the two did and still does lead at times to misunderstanding—especially when further work embracing a Marxian methodology and viewpoint is being undertaken. Hence Engels, who seems to have been at least implicitly and perhaps even explicitly aware of the distinction, attempted late in life in his letters on historical materialism to preclude a dogmatic interpretation of Marxian materialism.[50] For in actual fact, in detailed analyses such as *The 18th Brumaire of Louis Bonaparte,* which he in several of these letters recommends for the study of Marx's historical method, the ideological super-structure most definitely does play a role; only in broader analyses, such as that of *Capital,* can such features largely be ignored.

CHAPTER 5

The Young Marx: Observations on Humanism and Alienation

WE have already seen that Marx's early critique of Hegel provides an adequate basis for the understanding of his own methodology in all his subsequent work. There remains, however, the question of the positive doctrines of his early writings—especially those concerned with humanism and alienation—and their relation to his later theories. The major difficulty in dealing with this question is that the debate concerning it has been so highly politicized that its real substance is invariably lost in the smoke and fury of ideological battle. Though largely ignored when first published in Marx's *Complete Writings* in 1932, the *Economic and Philosophical Manuscripts of 1844*, which contain these doctrines, have in the last two decades become a great source of political controversy. Seen as an important political weapon by many leftist opponents of Stalinism, they were used by several East European intellectuals in an attempt to provide justification for demands for liberalization in their imperialized nations; less importantly, perhaps, but just as fervently, many social democrats such as Eric Fromm and Michael Harrington as well as some libertarian Marxist revolutionaries like Raya Duneyevska have also wielded them as a weapon in their respective struggles with Soviet ideology. Communist Party apologists such as Althusser in their turn have been at great pains to dissociate the early unpublished manuscripts from the Communist Party's official version of Marx, while, just as eagerly, anti-Communist ideologues like Daniel Bell have worked for the same end.[1] In the meantime, many non-Marxist humanists, including some of the more liberal clergy, have seen in the *Manuscripts* an opportunity for the "dialogue" with Marxists which they seem perpetually to be attempting, and have, in the course of arranging said dialogue, assimilated Marx, as thoroughly as an amoeba throwing out its pseudopods, to an undifferentiated humanistic protoplasm which can generate only a swirling confusion of marginally similar traditions, falsehoods, and half-truths. Finally, into this fracas and meeting of minds stepped many intellectuals of the new left and "counterculture" movements who found in the *Manuscripts* a possible theoretical framework for an understanding of the alienation and spiritual impoverishment which they observed in the modern capitalism they had recently rejected. Like the non-Marxist humanists, they tended to ignore the later theory and picked rather selectively from the early, ultimately incurring the wrath of Marxists of all schools.

With such a wide range of the political spectrum actively embroiled in these controversies, it is difficult not to let one's own political persuasions weigh too heavily on an examination of the evidence. To whatever extent possible I would like, however, to do just that. Though perhaps I am deceiving myself, I feel that I may have an advantage in accomplishing this insofar as, unlike the partisans described above, I find my attitude toward the *Manuscripts* relatively neutral; politically, I find I can glean little from them that cannot be found elsewhere in Marx, while my general viewpoint is that there is little of direct political—as opposed to theoretical—value in Marx at this date anyway. Long debates concerning what Marx would do in 1975, given his political position, seem to me to be as singularly unproductive as they are seductive, given, I suppose, the authoritarian mentality to which we are all heir. At any rate, the first order of the day, if we are going to avoid ideology and get a clear view of the early Marx with his observations on humanism and his theory of alienation in its relationship to his subsequent work, is to formulate clearly the questions to be asked about it. First, of course, what, if anything, is carried over into the later theory? Second, assuming that we find that something is, what is its function in the theory? Let us turn now to an account of the relevant portions of the *Manuscripts* to begin to answer these.

I   *The Account in the* Manuscripts

The *Economic and Philosophical Manuscripts* represent Marx's first attempt at the project which he brings to fruition in *Capital*, a critique of political economy. As such, though the central theme of the latter work, Marx's own version of the labor theory of value and its social implications, is not yet clearly in evidence, in spirit at least there is continuity between the works. Marx has in the *Manuscripts* already turned to the viewpoint which will occupy him as both scientist and politician for the rest of his life, and this viewpoint is as unequivocally present here as in the later critique; the nature of his understanding beginning from this viewpoint is, however, what is for us in question.

Marx begins his critique, as he himself observes, starting from the presuppositions of political economy itself. Having done so, he then turns to an account of its shortcomings from a position external to it. Its chief fault is, he notes, its failure to give a full explanation of the facts of capitalist economic life in that it is unable to grasp the internal dynamics of capitalism. Competition, wages, profits, even exchange itself are explained in terms of external and accidental conditions by the economists. To understand their real interconnections and wellsprings within capitalism itself, however, we have to turn to the relationship of the worker to production. Marx begins to look at this starting from what he refers to as "a *contemporary* economic fact":[2]

The worker becomes poorer the more wealth he produces and the more his production increases in power and extent. The worker becomes an ever cheaper commodity the more goods he creates. The *devaluation* of the human world increases in direct relation with the *increase in value* of the world of things. Labour does not only create goods; it also produces itself and the worker as a *commodity*, and indeed in the same proportion as it produces goods.

From this it follows that "the object produced by labour, its product, now stands opposed to it as an *alien being,* as a *power independent* of the producer." Likewise, the act of producing it is an activity of alienation, of alienating the product which "merely summarizes the alienation in the work activity itself." If we view the product, moreover, in the manner of Hegel, as an objectification of the worker's labor, that is, of himself, we see that in his objectified form he is his own enemy and the process of production whereby he objectifies and hence alienates himself is "an activity which is directed against him-

self, independent of him and not belonging to him," a forced
activity in every sense of the term. In failing to study the relationship between the worker and his production, political
economy has concealed from itself the concept from which its
categories can be derived. For this is what Marx will attempt
to demonstrate—not, he reminds us, as a philosophical exercise,
but, since the alienation of the worker and his production is an
"economic fact," as an analysis of this fact by way of an
analysis of the concept of alienated labor.[3]

We have seen so far the two primary aspects of the act of
alienation of labor:[4] (1) the worker's relation to his product
as an "alien object which dominates him"; (2) his relationship to
its production as an alien, involuntary, forced, depleating, self-
destructive, and unpossessed activity, a mere means of satisfaction
of needs, of no intrinsic worth in itself. The former, Marx remarks,
expands itself into a generalized alienation from nature—the
ground of all production—as a "hostile world"; the latter he characterizes as "self-alienation." From these two aspects still another
can be derived: (3) the alienation of man from his species-life
and hence, his species and his essence.[5] The concept of "species-
life" Marx takes from Feuerbach who, in his naturalistic and
humanistic inversion of Hegel, defines man as the only species
which is conscious of itself as a species, that is, conscious of its
species-life and its development, a quality which gives it uni-
versality in its particularity; this quality Feuerbach calls man's
"species-being." For Marx, unlike Feuerbach whom he sees as
concentrating exclusively on contemplative consciousness, "the
practical construction of an *objective world, the manipulation*
of inorganic nature, is the confirmation of man as a conscious
species-being, i.e., a being who [after Feuerbach] treats the
species as his own being or himself as a species-being." For man
alone among animals produces, not in an instinct-determined
"single direction," but "universally," freely, and consciously,
making nature appear as "his work and his reality" molded to
his judgments of need and aesthetic value. "The object of labour
is, therefore," Marx concludes, "the *objectification of man's
species-life*" in which he reproduces himself "actively and in a
real sense, and . . . sees his own reflection in a world which he
has constructed." It is the concrete manifestation of his species

consciousness. In a social situation in which man as laborer is alienated, however, both, via (1), from nature and the changes he works in it and, via (2), from himself in the form of his own life's productive activity, he is alienated likewise from his species-life, that is, from his species. The activity which expresses his species-life, moreover, cannot be viewed by him as such an expression, but is seen rather, as we observed above, as merely the means for sustaining his individual life; if being a species-being is his essence, he is thus estranged from that essence. The division of labor is the form which human activity as species-activity takes under these conditions of species estrangement; it is "the economic expression of the *social character of labour* within alienation."[6]

From the above and the foregoing aspects of alienation of labor it furthermore follows as "a direct consequence" that (4) "*man* is *alienated* from other *men*." In confronting himself, man, since his being is social, necessarily confronts others; thus, in being estranged from himself, he is necessarily estranged from others as well; he is forced to regard them "according to the standards and relationships in which he finds himself placed as a worker."[7] Finally, at a point farther along in the text, Marx mentions still another aspect of alienation resulting from labor's alienation from its production: (5) the whole social world is ruled by "an inhuman power."[8] This, he notes, estranges the capitalist as well as the worker, since it is a general condition of capitalist society from either's point of view.

But as yet in this account we do not even have the capitalist. In order to introduce him, we must turn to Marx's derivation of private property from alienated labor: If the product and the activity which produces it are both alien to the worker and do not belong to him, observes Marx, then they must belong to another. In the earliest stages of "advanced production" in Egypt, India, and Mexico it was in fact taken to belong to the gods; but even there this notion was a mere facade which covered the reality. In reality, "if the product of labour does not belong to the worker, but confronts him as an alien power, this can only be because it belongs to *a man other than the worker*." Whenever a man is "related to his own activity as to unfree activity . . . he is related to it as activity in the service, and under the domination, coercion and yoke, of another man." Alienated labor thus coexists with private property in all its forms, both capitalist and precapitalist.[9] It is in fact presupposed by the institution of private property; private property is a "consequence" of it.

Marx is not here speaking merely of the fact that it is derived from the concept of alienation in his analysis. Rather he sees it as explanatorily posterior in a causal sense. In the same way that "the gods are *fundamentally* not the cause but the product of confusions of human reason," so also is private property not the cause but the product of alienated labor. For the institution of private property has not descended from the heavens on mankind, but is the result of relations among men, namely, those which alienate the worker from his production. When one deals with labor "one deals directly with mankind itself," the actual subject of mankind's institutions, while in dealing with property per se theorists erroneously take themselves "to be dealing with something external to mankind." Thus, to see property rooted in relations of labor is to see it as the human institution which it is; to study the development of labor's alienation is the key to understanding the development of property.[10] This formulation, however, must not be read too rigidly, as eventually there is a "reciprocal influence" between the institution and the social relations in which it is grounded.

Like private property, wages, which are attendant to it in its capitalist form, are also consequences of alienated labor. This leads Marx to observe that "an enforced *increase in wages* . . . would be nothing more than a *better remuneration of slaves,* and would not restore, either to the worker or to the work, their human significance and worth." An equality of incomes in the manner of P. J. Proudhon would likewise not change the fundamental relation of alienation but merely reduce everyone to the status of the contemporary worker and make society into "an abstract capitalist."[11] This, nonetheless, is for Marx here in the *Manuscripts,* as we have already seen, a necessary first stage in the development of the communism which will finally abolish alienation, while the reduction of everyone to the status of worker is, moreover, seen as necessary in the transition in all his subsequent works.

Though alienation, as we have seen, gives rise to all forms of private property, it reaches its full development, as in consequence so does also private property itself, only in its capitalist form. Here alone its "secret" is revealed. For only in this form does labor lose all vestiges of "social meaning" with the stripping away of property's "political and social disguise."[12] Whereas in previous forms—apparently even slave societies—property relations, being still mediated by social institutions, are not as openly expressions of alienation, under capitalism they reveal themselves in all their brittleness. The laborer exists for capital only as a laborer; the products of labor confront him "as *capital*, in which every natural and social characteristic of the object is *dissolved* . . . in which the *same* capital remains the *same* in the most varied natural and social conditions, which have no relevance to its *real* content." Private property under such conditions "no longer even *appears* to be connected with human relationships"; the alienation which it expresses has reached its zenith. Its supercession is hence close at hand. The increasing domination of society by capital is inextricably linked to an "increasing alienation which hastens its own abolition."[13]

This account of capitalist society finds its echo in the *Communist Manifesto*'s references to capitalism as tearing away the "veils of sentiment" of the feudal social forms:[14]

The bourgeoisie, wherever it has got the upper hand, has put an end to all feudal, patriarchal, idyllic relations. It has pitilessly torn asunder the motley feudal ties that bound man to his "natural superiors," and has left remaining no other nexus between man and man than naked self-interest, than callous "cash payment." It has drowned the most heavenly ecstasies of religious fervor, of chivalrous enthusiasm, of Philistine sentimentalism in the icy water of egotistical calculation. It has resolved personal worth into exchange value and, in place of the numberless indefeasible chartered freedoms, has set up that single unconscionable freedom—free trade. In one word, for exploitation, veiled by religious and political illusions, it has substituted naked, shameless, direct, brutal exploitation.

It also reverberates in the discussion of the fetishism of commodities in the first chapter of *Capital*. Here, however, as we shall see, the reduction of social relations to commercial relations seems to carry with it none of the apocalyptic charge that it did in the *Manuscripts*—or even the *Manifesto,* for that matter. In neither of these two later returns to theme, it should also here be noted, is reference made to alienation.

As private property is the expression—Marx says "the material and sensuous expression"—of alienated human life, its supercession will likewise be the supercession of this alienation; it is thus "the appropriation of *human* life . . . and the return of man from religion, the family, the state, etc. to his *human,* i.e., social life."[15] For these institutions are "only *particular* forms of production [under alienation] and come under its general law"; they are, that is, subordinate to the alienated labor/private property complex and subsumed under this general relation.[16] Once nonalienated social life is established and life for men has become fully human, not only will these alienated forms vanish, but nature also will itself be transformed for men and take on "human significance." For, as we noted already previously, it now for man will no longer be an alien object which oppresses him, but the basis of his union with others in society —even in those cases where his work itself must in its nature be solitary; society will become "the accomplished union of man with nature, the veritable resurrection of nature, the realized naturalism of man and the realized humanism of nature." Under these conditions even human needs themselves will be altered. "Private property," says Marx "has made us so stupid and partial that an object is only *ours* when we have it, when it exists for us as capital or when it is directly eaten, drunk, worn, inhabited, etc., in short *utilized* in some way"; but when the world has become human for us, need will have lost its "egoistic character" just as "nature [will have] lost its mere *utility* by the fact that its utilization has become *human* utilization" and every relation we have to it will be a far more subtle "appropriation of human reality" than the mere possession which we now know; even our sufferings will thus be transformed. The senses, both "physical and intellectual," will be emancipated. Not only will human sensibility—the "so-called spiritual senses" and the "practical senses (desiring, loving, etc.)" as well as the five senses—be for the first time able to develop fully, aesthetically, but also "the senses and minds of other men [will] have become

my *own* appropriation." For the individual, being in reality a
social being, feels himself, in his individuality and because of
it, isolated only in that he is alienated from his species-life; in
reality "individual life and species-life are not different things.
... Though man is a unique individual—and it is just his particularity which makes him an individual, a really *individual*
communal being—he is equally the *whole*, the ideal whole, the
subjective existence of society as thought and experienced." The
species exists in its subjective aspect only through its members.

In summing up this line of discussion, before turning to the
question of methodology which we examined in the last chapter,
Marx writes as follows:[17]

Let us assume *man* to be *man*, and his relation to the world to be
a human one. Then love can only be exchanged for love, trust for
trust, etc. If you wish to enjoy art you must be an artistically
cultivated person; if you wish to influence other people you must be
a person who really has a stimulating and encouraging effect upon
others. Every one of your relations to man and to nature must be
a *specific expression*, corresponding to the object of your will, of
your *real individual* life. If you love without evoking love in return,
i.e., if you are not able, by the *manifestation* of yourself as a loving
person, to make yourself a *beloved person*, then your love is impotent
and a misfortune.

Communism as fully developed is thus seen to be the quintes-
sence of individual responsibility—a far cry from the enforced
conformity with which the popular mind has often, especially
in the America of the Cold War era, associated it.

On the other hand, elements which serve to confirm these
dystopian fantasies are, as we have seen, apparently thought by
the Marx of the *Manuscripts* to be possible, if not inevitable,
in the first stages of communist development. In fact, the *Manuscripts* provide the only source in Marx which can legitimately
be said to fuel the fires of such fantasy. It is ironical in a way,
especially when we recall that the *Manuscripts* also provide the
sole reference to the possibility of some sort of political despotism
in communism's first phases, that so many humanists and liber-
tarians have struggled so hard to show them somehow central
to Marxism. In his subsequent work—perhaps through his real

contacts with the developing workers' movement of which he was relatively ignorant at the time he composed the *Manuscripts* —Marx seems clearly far more confident that a humane and reasonable proletarian governance of society can be instituted.

Finally, before turning to an examination of the material here presented, we should note a second function—in addition to that of intensification of the alienation of labor—which capitalism in the *Manuscripts* account performs in the development of the preconditions for the supercession of alienated life, namely, that of producing the material prerequisites for this supercession in that it develops industry to a level undreamed of previously while, as Marx puts it, "only through developed industry, i.e., through the mediation of private property [fully developed or capitalist private property], does the ontological essence of human passions, in its totality and its humanity, come into being."[18]

II *The* Manuscripts' *Relation to Marx's Later Work*

If we now return to our initial question—namely, what if anything, of this material on alienation survives in Marx's later work?—our answer seems to be that, in a certain sense, all of it does. That is to say, all of the five aspects of alienation which Marx describes can unquestionably be found in his later writings, though they are not there necessarily categorized under this concept—and, in fact, after the 1858 "Grundrisse" draft of *Capital*, are almost never found so categorized. The first, the alienation of the worker from his product and his consequent subjection to it encompasses in the *Manuscripts* those class relations which, under capitalism as well as other class societies, keep the producer from controlling what he produces and, specifically under capitalism, make him subject to the vicissitudes of the market. This theme, though worked out both somewhat differently and far more profoundly in the later work, is endemic to all of Marx's writings from the time he first embraces socialism to his death. In the same manner, the theme of socialism as the remedy for this condition is everywhere present in his writings, a fact which must already be clear to the reader. The second aspect, the self-alienation of the worker in his productive activity like-

wise finds its echo everywhere in Marx; much of *Capital* in fact
is devoted to an examination of the forced, depleting nature of
work under capitalism.[19] Moreover, in the *Critique of the Gotha
Program,* we find him speaking of work in the "higher phase
of communist society" as having lost this characteristic and
"become not only a means of life but life's prime want."[20]

The third aspect, species alienation's presence in subsequent
writings, is by far the most problematic. Though the phenomena
which characterize its supercession can most certainly be detected
in *Capital* and other later sources' descriptions of the higher
stages of communist society as a voluntary association of producers in which society becomes a self-conscious human process,
etc., it seems to make no easily identifiable appearance in the
later discussion of capitalism itself. We might, of course, want
to maintain that, insofar as it was derived by Marx from the
first two aspects of alienation, it is embodied along with them
in whatever kind of continued presence we finally take them to
have in this discussion; but the difficulty in doing so can easily
be seen once we notice that its derivation was dependent on the
characterization of the phenomena subsumed under these aspects
as aspects of the alienation of labor; when this framework is
dropped—as it progressively is in Marx's subsequent work—the
derivation cannot go through. If we object here on the grounds
that, were it to turn out that the dropping of the alienation
framework with respect to the two primary aspects were only
nominal—a mere change in terminology—in Marx's later work,
then a hidden form of species alienation would necessarily also
be there present, we need only be reminded that the framework
is not in itself sufficient to validate the derivation anyway. The
further assumptions that man has a species-life and that it is
embodied in his collective productive activity are also needed;
only under these conditions does alienation from productive life
entail alienation from species. For this reason, unless we can
find such disguised evidence for species alienation or the phenomena subsumed under it in the later work, we are in no
way bound to assume it is there—and it is such evidence that,
as I said above, I fail anywhere to discover.

The last two aspects, like the two primary ones, present no
such problems. The alienation of man from man is exemplified

in class relations generally; it is further exacerbated under capitalism by what Marx takes to be the necessity of competition in this social form, both among the bourgeois and, to a lesser extent as the labor movement develops—but nonetheless still always in evidence—among the workers themselves who must vie for an increasingly insufficient number of jobs. The alienation due to the fact that an inhuman power governs social relations finds its correlate, like the alienation of the worker from his product, in the discussion of class societies everywhere in Marx. Both of these phenomena, moreover, however they are characterized, will on Marx's view vanish with the full development of communism.[21]

If the existence of some continuing presence of notions which were in the *Economic and Philosophical Manuscripts* developed via the Marxian theory of alienation is all that the defenders of the Young Marx are maintaining, then their case is easily proven.[22] If, however, they hold in answer to the second question with which we began—namely, What is the role of alienation in Marx's later work?—that this role is constant throughout—even where the terminology of the theory is no longer present—then, as our above comments have already indicated, their claim is false. For, since it seems that species alienation or the alienation of the human essence is nowhere detectable in Marx's later accounts of capitalism or its development toward its supercession, it certainly plays no role at all in them. On the other hand, insofar as it is one aspect of the alienation of labor, in the 1844 *Manuscripts* it does; for, as we have seen in the exposition of alienated labor in the previous section of this chapter, as it intensifies in all its aspects with the increasing domination of society by capitalism it becomes the lever for the supercession of capitalism.[23] The later account cannot therefore be a mere presentation of the earlier decked out in new terminology, as many of the defenders of the Young Marx are wont to feel it is; one aspect of alienation having vanished completely in the meantime, there must be *some* substantial, and not simply nominal, modification of the theory of capitalist development in the later work.

Remembering that species alienation as an aspect of alienated labor depends not only on the two primary aspects of alienation

but also on man's being seen as actually having a species-life
or essential nature—that is, intrinsic transhistorical needs which
must be fulfilled if he is to exist in a fully human fashion—we
might be tempted to assume that it is this notion in its entirety
which he drops in his later work. In fact, it seems, however, that
he does not. Rather it is only the more specific notion that
species-being, as understood in the *Manuscripts*, is man's essence
which appears to be missing in later work; for, though, as stated
above, phenomena associated with the abolition of this species-
being alienation survive in Marx's descriptions of communism,
there is no indication in anything which he says that he continues to think of them as the fulfillment of an essence or the
supercession of an alienated species-life.[24] Despite this there
is a more modest assumption concerning a human essence which
survives—or perhaps replaces this original view of human nature
—in Marx. This is the notion that to be fulfilled as a human it
is necessary to express one's creativity freely in all the manifold
forms it can take.[25] When human nature is viewed in this way,
communism becomes not so much the fulfillment of human
nature—as it is when human nature is characterized as species-
being—rather, it is the *prerequisite* for the fulfillment of man's
essence. Thus, in a passage we have already cited from *The
German Ideology*, Marx writes that "personal freedom" as opposed to what "has up till now been called personal freedom"
depends upon communism which alone makes possible "the
means of cultivating . . . [one's] gifts in all directions"; while,
in an also previously cited passage from the first volume of
Capital, we likewise find "the fully developed individual" of
communism with his variety of skills compared to the "mere
fragment of a man" that exists under capitalism.

It is not clear, however, what role exactly the human essence
of this later view plays as an *explanatory device* in Marxian
theory, i.e., how closely analogous it is to that played by the
essence conceived as species-being in the 1844 *Manuscripts*. In
the above passage from *Capital*, for example, Marx in no way
attributes the abolition of the division of labor to the human
essence; it is instead seen as necessitated by the rapid technological development of modern industry; the creation of fully
human conditions of production is itself presented as a *result*

only—perhaps even a happy accident. *The German Ideology* discussion, on the other hand, appears to treat it as an actual felt
need of the proletarians once the contradiction between productive forces and social relations has become apparent; as
such it is a force among others leading to revolutionary change.
This view seems also to be reflected in the ninth point of the
Manifesto's general political program, which aims at the abolition of the distinction between agricultural and industrial labor.
Of course, *The German Ideology* is itself a quite early work,
written less than two years after the 1844 *Manuscripts* themselves, as is also the *Communist Manifesto*, relative to *Capital*
at least. Perhaps then it would seem we should view human
nature as ceasing to play a role for Marx in the dynamics of
historical development once his understanding of social dynamics
reached its full maturity. This view is rendered less plausible,
however, once we note that the increasingly mechanical role
given to the worker as industry develops is undoubtedly thought
by Marx—throughout his career—to have a function in the intensification of struggle—though he may, as the *Capital* passage may or
may not indicate, have found that role relatively less important
as he studied the class struggle further. More trivial yet in its
presence perhaps, but nonetheless always to be found in Marx
is the realization that, no matter how one is socialized—leaving
aside for the moment the question of variety in one's work—
certain working conditions in themselves are difficult to tolerate;[26]
to the extent therefore that capitalism is forced to maintain
such inhuman conditions this is a factor in the struggle between
capital and labor as well.

So clearly the function of a human essence has not entirely
atrophied in later Marxian theory, though its role has certainly
diminished. It has, moreover, we should note, become simpler
in becoming less central as well. In the *Manuscripts* it acts as
a kind of subliminal force manifesting itself in a variety of ways.
Though envy and impoverishment are there the main motives
we detect in the proletariat's establishment of the crude beginnings of communism, even so, he tells us, "communism . . . is
already aware of being the reintegration of man, his return to
himself, the supercession of man's self-alienation."[27] The form
which this awareness takes is perhaps still "contaminated by

private property" but it is present nonetheless. In contrast, the more modest assumptions about human nature in the later work relate more directly to motivation and behavior; the more highly theoretical concepts which Marx now employs deal, as we have to some extent in the second chapter already seen, with social and economic phenomena rather than the human essence as an overarching force.

Althusser's claim that "in 1845 [the date of the composition of the "Theses on Feuerbach"], Marx broke radically with every theory that based history and politics on an essence of man" is, of course, an exaggeration.[28] The text of the sixth thesis, which he relies on heavily to support this dating of the above "radical break," does not, moreover, carry the implications which he thinks it does, and hence lends no real support to his claim. When Marx says in criticism of Feuerbach in this thesis that "the human essence is no abstraction inherent in each single individual" but that "in its reality it is the ensemble of the social relations," he is not setting down a full-blown social relativism; he is merely objecting to Feuerbach's ahistorical approach to the human essence, as the remainder of the thesis clearly indicates. Feuerbach, due to his failure to think historically, is forced "to abstract [in Hegel's sense of isolating the part from the whole] from the historical process and to fix the religious sentiment as something by itself, and to presuppose an abstract–*isolated*–human individual. . . . The human essence, therefore, can with him be comprehended only as 'species,' as an internal, dumb generality which merely *naturally* unites the many individuals."[29] The true human essence, on the contrary, is to be understood only in the context of human history. Neither is the existence of this essence anywhere denied—in fact its existence is asserted—nor is it in any clear sense denied that the essence in question might be the species-being of the *Manuscripts* of the year previous itself. Marx criticizes Feuerbach's essence of man for being understood only as species in the sense of an extrasocial characteristic, but his own conception of species-being is not subject to such a criticism; crude as might be their handling in comparison with his later analyses, both the social and the historical nature of the science of man are recognized already by Marx in 1844; essence is never by him treated in isolation from either.

Despite all this, it is nonetheless true, as we have already seen, that human essence in alienation (unfulfilled and moving toward fulfillment) most definitely has both a diminished and a different role in the later theory; the concepts which replace it, moreover, though they may be looked upon as a development *from* the other aspects of alienation dealt with in the *Manuscripts,* are not a mere reiteration of these. They are many of them new concepts completely, and the injection of these (for example, the notions of productive forces and productive relations) into the theory, combined with the above alteration in the function which human nature plays in it, certainly gives Marx's later work a qualitatively different feel;[30] to deny the striking difference in both quality and profundity between the analysis of *Capital* and that of the *Economic and Philosophical Manuscripts* would in fact be folly. That such folly is nonetheless committed can only be understood when we recognize that Marx as a social theorist has—wrongly I believe—lost prestige in the eyes of many today even as, often among the same people, Marxism as an ideological weapon proliferates like religious fervor in a time of plague.

This is not, however, to say that the theory of alienation is necessarily a mere piece of ideology—"ethics" or "philosophical [as opposed to empirical] anthropology"—as a critic like Althusser claims. Certainly any view which posits an essence as dynamic is teleological in the limited sense of being functionalist in structure, but functionalist analyses are not inherently unscientific. They only become so if we can establish that the goal which the function in question is to fulfill is not in some way objectively present, a need for example, but a mere normative objective imposed by the theoretician himself. As such, functionalist theories do tend to be problematic, and this is perhaps the major reason why Marx reduces his use of functionalist elements as his work goes on; to see humans as generally debilitated by prolonged mechanical activity and necessarily resistant to personally senseless dangers is not excessively controversial, while to posit a subliminal need for communalism in production may be.

The terminology of alienation seems to persist longer in Marx's work than its essential theoretical function. Thus, though at least one reference to it is found in *The German Ideology*, it does no particular work there and seems to function more as a figure of speech rather than a real theoretical device.[31] Its use is more extensive in the "Grundrisse" notes for *Capital* which Marx worked up twelve years later; but here again its real integration into the theoretical dynamic seems nonexistent. The same can be said for the occasional reference to "estrangement" or "alienation" which we find in *Capital* itself. Many elements found in the theory, as noted, have nonetheless passed under other descriptions into subsequent work, at times becoming so integrated with novel elements as to defy abstraction from them. The objectification of social relations under capitalism in particular will prove central to the later analysis of *Capital*, as the discussion of the next chapter will reveal.

CHAPTER 6

On Marx's Capital:
The Critique of Political Economy

MARX intended *Capital* to be a work of four volumes. The first volume, the only one fully prepared for publication and published during his life, is entitled "The Process of Capitalist Production." It provides a general account of this process, a first approximation, somewhat idealized—in a manner which resembles in some ways, but not all, the manner in which the ideal gas laws of physics are idealizations of reality—as well as a history of the development of the process. The second volume, "The Process of Circulation of Capital," deals with the further question of the various movements of capital within the system of capitalist production; and the third volume, "The Process of Capitalist Production as a Whole," integrates the first two, correcting earlier idealizations. These latter two volumes were published by Engels from more or less complete drafts after Marx's death; the fourth volume, the manuscript for which has been published in English under the title, "Theories of Surplus Value," is far less finished; it deals with developments in political economy, the science of economics itself rather than with the capitalist system directly, filling out in a more detailed and explicit fashion the avowed intent of the work's subtitle that it be "A Critique of Political Economy."[1]

To try to deal with all aspects of a work this large in a book the scope of this one is clearly impossible. In the following I have therefore limited myself to presenting some basic features of the theory of capitalist society as developed by Marx in *Capital* with an eye to presenting selected consequences of and problems in the theory which I feel to be the most interesting from a contemporary viewpoint. In doing so, I have almost entirely disregarded questions concerning the circulation of

121

capital. I have also ignored historical questions of capitalist development, but refer the reader back to the account, in large part taken from the first volume of *Capital*, given in the second chapter of this book.

I *The Structure of the Capitalist Economy*

If one were to take an overview of capitalist society in order to contrast it with its predecessors, whatever else one might want to say about it, two striking facts could hardly be overlooked. First, in it, laborers, no longer bound by traditional relations of servitude, are hired by employers or owners (that is, capitalists) for wages in order that they might work to produce a profit for the employer. Second, to a far greater extent than ever before in history, goods in capitalist societies take the form of commodities. The wealth of capitalist societies "presents itself," to use Marx's own words, "as an immense accumulation of commodities, its unit being a single commodity," namely, money or precious metals as money.[2]

It is convenient to begin an account of Marx's analysis of capitalism as developed in *Capital* with an attempt to understand what he sees as necessary if we are to explain the existence of these two easily agreed upon facts.[3] What, asks Marx, is the nature of a commodity, and how does production of commodities using free wage labor result in profits for the employer of the labor? Let us start by looking at his answer to the first of these questions. To begin, in order to be a commodity an item must have "use value" or utility, that is, it must be something that people want; for this, as Marx notes in several places, is the real basis, the "substance" of wealth. Still, though a necessary condition for its being a commodity, use value is, of course, hardly a sufficient one; the items produced by *any* society are, except under extraordinary circumstances, useful to members of the society in the terms in which they define their needs, and many useful items are such that one would never—though, with contemporary ecological problems, I hesitate to use the word "never"—think to treat them as commodities, for example, sunshine and air. This brings us to the second and sufficient characteristic of a commodity, its exchange value, the fact that one can and does set a value on the item at which it can be exchanged for another *or,* what comes to the same thing, exchanged for money in the same amount as another. Use value is a difficult thing to quantify and, though most contemporary economists attempt to do so, they carry out such quantification only with reference to the value of exchange, the quantification of which we see every day all around us. But what is the basis of exchange value?

The immediate answer that those of us trained in the present-day educational system might be inclined to give is that the value of exchange is determined by the relation of the supply of the item in question to the demand which exists for it. A moment's reflection, however, will reveal the inadequacy of using ratios of supply to demand as such a basis. Though prices, at least in an economy of pure competition, certainly do undergo short term fluctuations on the basis of this ratio, over any sizeable period, as long as the scarcities involved are not absolute, supply and demand will tend to equalize as capital investment is withdrawn from areas with small demand and oversupply and placed in those with scarce supply and great demand. If shirts, for example, are in oversupply while automobiles are scarce, new investment will go into the latter and not the former until the inventory of oversupplied shirts is used up and they begin to sell at their former price again. The question then is, when this has occurred, when supply and demand have been equalized, what is it that determines exchange value? Or, to put the matter slightly differently, what determines the basic exchange value around which prices fluctuate according to the ratio of supply to demand?

The answer which Marx gives to this question is that it is "human labour in the abstract," which is to say, labor as human activity without regard to the specific form the activity takes, that is, without regard to whether it is weaving, or mining or what-have-you with which we are to be concerned. As such it can be measured quantitatively with respect to time alone.[4] To arrive at this answer Marx presents the reader with a short demonstration: If one quarter of corn and one x hundredweight of iron are equated, they must have some property in common which allows their equation via it. It cannot be a natural property, since they have no natural properties in common or, if they

do, these interest us only with respect to the commodities'
utilities (for example, the similarities between shale and petro-
leum are of interest to us insofar as the same products can be
extracted from them). But, as far as exchange value is concerned,
utility or use value is irrelevant just so long as the item concerned has it. From the point of view of exchange "one use-
value is just as good as another, provided that it be present in
sufficient quantity."[5] This leaves only one candidate for the property common to both—*viz.*, the human labor embodied in them.

Despite the seemingly *a priori* character of this demonstration,
the theory to which it points, namely, the labor theory of value,
is not—as we shall see and as the chapter on method has already
indicated—in any sense a metaphysical theory.[6] It is empirical
and held by Marx to be proved in practice, a scientific theory
of how capitalist social relations work. As such, it is, furthermore,
in no sense to be taken as ethical or ideological in any degree.
It in no way claims that labor is the creator of real worth or
wealth, since it deals only with the value of exchange and not
at all with utility, the substance of wealth; thus it does not
entail an ideology of labor. In its fully developed form in fact
communist society, as we have seen, will not use labor-time as
a measure for the distribution of goods at all.

Before proceeding to our second question concerning the
relation between wage labor and profit, some further common
misunderstandings regarding the labor theory should be examined. It is, to begin with, a frequent charge that, by making
human labor the sole depository of value, Marx fails to account for the role of technology in the capitalist economy. Do
not, it is often asked, machines produce value as well? Part of
the motivation for this question may rest on a confusion between
use value and exchange value; for surely machinery, by increasing
social productivity, increases social wealth. From the point
of view of exchange, however, this increased productivity is
not a *direct* concern, a fact which, as we shall see, leads capital,
according to Marx, into its fundamental dialectical contradiction. Still, however, even from the viewpoint of exchange value
increased productivity, whatever its causes, technological or
organizational, most certainly does have a bearing on exchange.
The abstract labor or labor-time to which Marx refers in the

labor theory of value is the *socially necessary* labor-time in any given branch of industry at any specific time. He in no way means to imply, he reminds the reader, that "the more idle and unskilful the labourer, the more valuable would his commodity be, because more time would be required in its production."[7] When powerlooms were introduced on a commercial basis in England, cutting in half the production time of cloth, the labor of the English handloom weavers "fell to one-half its former value." The level of productivity of machinery is a presupposition in the calculation of labor-time for purposes of exchange. To a lesser extent also machinery enters the calculation insofar as the labor-time embodied in the production and maintenance of the machine in question always enters the calculation of value. So it hardly can be charged to the theory that it emphasizes labor—and, by implication, the laborer—and ignores his machine, even after we are clear as to what sort of value we are talking about. Once again, to see the theory as embodying a hidden morality—as such a charge does—is a mistake.

Second, it is sometimes thought that Marx—again there being a suspicion of a hidden ideology in the theory—fails to take into account the differences between skilled and unskilled labor in his equation of value and abstract labor. He is, however, quite clear in drawing this distinction. Though the notion of abstract labor makes no distinction between working a lathe and digging a ditch in that abstract labor is purely quantitative, measured in units of socially necessary time, the allocation of units of labor time to a product presupposes a distinction between "simple average labour," the labor which in a given society on the average requires no special training, and skilled labor.[8] This latter is calculated as a multiple of simple labor, not merely in some theoretical sense but in practice constantly "by a process that goes on behind the backs of the producers" and hence appears "fixed by custom." The tendency in capitalism, that is to say, is to reduce labor always to a kind of lowest common denominator; it is a tendency realized in actuality more fully as the system develops and really *does* produce a mass work force of interchangeable operatives, but it is a tendency inherent even in capitalism's earliest stages in capital's view of labor.[9] Given the truth of this, Marx notes that we can "for simplicity's sake" ignore this reduction and treat all labor as simple, saving "ourselves the trouble of making the reduction."

Finally, it has at times been charged that counterinstances to the labor theory can be found in the exchange value of art works, patents, and other unique items of social utility. This is, of course, true, and Marx was explicit in his awareness of it as early as the 1847 *Poverty of Philosophy*;[10] but, as he notes, it is hardly the case that such items form the norm in capitalist society; hence, they do not in any measure determine the basis for capitalist exchange. Marx's analysis of capitalism is not aimed at uncovering a definition, against which even the most obscure counterinstance is telling; it is aimed at the actual determining relations of capitalist society.

Items sold under monopolistic conditions would, of course, as already noted in passing, also play havoc with value as labor, since they need not allow the free movement of investment to equalize supply to demand ratios. In this way, they too fail to be freely duplicable just as are commodities which are unique. "When we refer to a monopoly price," writes Marx, "we mean in general a price determined only by the purchasers' eagerness to buy and ability to pay, independent of the price determined by...the value of the products."[11] Again, in a somewhat different context, we find him claiming that commodity prices cannot correspond with their exchange values under conditions of either "natural or artificial monopoly."[12] Although, as we will see, the dynamic of his theory points toward the *development of* monopolies, his point of departure would thus seem to be the classical laissez-faire capitalism of his time. However, lest we hold to this viewpoint too rigidly, it should be added that a situation of limited monopoly, when considered by Marx from the point of view of the system as a whole, "would merely transfer a portion of the profit of the other commodity-producers to the commodities having the monopoly price" while leaving the law of value for the total system intact.[13] The limited role of monopoly in the system does not thus alter its overall features, though it does call for adjustments within it.

Let us turn now to our second question—*viz.*, How does commodity production using wage labor result in profit? It might at first seem that in the "free" transaction, bound only by contract, by which the laborer hires himself out to the employer, it is his labor that he sells and that the employer buys. Many common expressions, the "price of labor," the "value of one's labor," etc., serve in fact to reinforce this belief.[14] If it were true, however, that labor is what is bought and sold, the employer would pay out to the laborer exactly what the laborer embodied in the commodity he produced for the employer and there would be no way, under the labor theory, to explain profits—other than the unlikely thesis that they result from the employer's own expenditure of labor.[15] Labor, if treated as itself a commodity, can only exchange for its own value in other commodities, as happens in the case of straight-forward bartering or sales in craft and rural markets by the producers themselves; the sale of a product, once completed, cannot itself miraculously produce more value (labor) in it. If, however, the commodity which a laborer sells when he hires out is, not his labor, but his *ability* to labor, "his labor-power," then the mystery of profit is easily solved. For all the employer must now do in order to reap a profit is pay less for this commodity than the value he derives from it. And, Marx points out, if we consider what determines the value of any commodity, namely, the labor socially necessary to produce it, we can see that this can be easily done. For the value of labor-power is "the labour-time necessary for the production, and consequently also the reproduction" of it, that is, the labor time necessary to provide sustenance, a livelihood, for the laborers and the off-spring they must rear in order to replenish the work force.[16] And this is exactly what workers' wages do. What constitutes such sustenance will vary from one place and time to another, the minimum limit being always "those means of subsistence that are physically indispensable" to renew the laborer's "vital energy" so that he can work efficiently.

Thus, if the worker and his family can subsist on goods equal in value to the value he produces in six hours and he works ten, six hours worth of value will constitute his wage and four hours worth of value (four hours of labor-time) will be available as surplus, that is, profit, for the owners of capital.[17] What the laborer "hires out" is quite literally himself; common

usage here is—perhaps because it is more personal and presented from the laborer's viewpoint—far less concealing of the
actual state of affairs than it is in talk of the "price of labor."
The appropriation of surplus by the capitalist is called by Marx
the "exploitation" of labor.

Despite my many previous arguments that the theory is not a
piece of ideology, this choice of terms may seem to belie
any such contention. Though it surely is in some sense a
technical concept, it would be patently absurd to maintain
that the concept of exploitation as used here is merely that.
Moreover, the partisan sentiments of the above-mentioned reference to exploitation are hardly a unique occurrence in Marx's
work. Anyone with the least familiarity with *Capital* cannot
fail to notice Marx's sense of outrage, expressed usually in a
delicious irony, and seemingly integral with the rest of the
body of his text. How then are we to understand this open
incursion of moral sentiment into theory if the theory is to be
understood as social science, as I maintain? I believe we can
without too much difficulty, if we recall Marx's contention that
all ideology, including morality, reflects class interests; although
a ruling class will always present its ideology as universal and
will, to one extent or another, perpetuate such beliefs also in
the classes it subjugates, it cannot be universal—nor can *any*
ideology developed in a class society—simply because the class
antagonisms of the society make it time and again implausible
to maintain any such claim. People are ultimately bound to
their needs and, in any social situation in which the needs
of one class are necessarily at odds with those of another,
this fact cannot be fully glossed over. From the proletarian
viewpoint the appropriation of surplus by the capitalist *is*
exploitation. And Marx is writing from such a viewpoint.

This viewpoint, lest the reader misunderstand, is not to be
equated necessarily with that of any given proletarian or group
of proletarians at any given time. It is the viewpoint of the
class itself, of the proletariat's interests when its real situation—
the struggle it inevitably and constantly carries on—is fully
and clearly revealed. The ethics which Marx presupposes in
Capital reflects these class interests even as the science of
the book reveals what they are. The working class, of course,

need not adopt this or any other ethic in order to engage in or intensify the class struggle; class interest precedes class ideology and a class' situation determines its interest. Marx, as I have already said, in no way intends this highly complex work to be propaganda. Furthermore, it should be kept in mind that to see the real situation of the proletariat does not necessarily commit one to its viewpoint—unless, of course, one is a proletarian—and a middle-class revolutionist such as Marx or a bourgeois one like Engels must take the side in the class struggle which he does by a choice determined in a more personal and complex way.

The real situation of the proletariat can, however, be seen much more easily from the side of the proletariat. There is, moreover, Marx feels, no symmetry between this fact and the clarity of knowledge provided from the side of capital; the real situation of capital is *not* seen easily from capital's position. Capital's position is a position which, beyond a certain point, necessarily distorts; the capitalist or ideologue of capitalism must shed his established ideology in order to see the social reality whereas, from the position of the proletariat, both the proletarian situation and, since it only exists in dialectical interaction with capital, the capitalists' situation as well, can be clearly understood; in short, the whole of capitalism reveals itself most easily and clearly from an investigation launched from the position of commitment to the proletariat, and the fully developed proletarian viewpoint or ethic reveals itself together with the revelation of the underlying facts of bourgeois social life.

The question still remains as to why the bourgeois viewpoint, that is, bourgeois ideology, rather than coinciding with a penetration of the inner workings of capitalism as does the proletarian viewpoint, in fact inhibits the development of such insight. The answer to this, it turns out, is actually implicit in the Marxian theory of value as we have examined it so far. The fact and nature of surplus in the dominant modes of previous class-structured societies was never concealed. On the feudal manor, for example, "every serf knows that what he expends in the service of his lord is a definite quantity of his own personal labour-power."[18] He produces by his labor a certain sum of goods, uses a portion of them for his and his offsprings' sustenance, and gives up the remainder to lord and clergy. The official ideology, of course, assures him that he is only fulfilling his function in a God-ordained hierarchy; the exploitation of the serf is, as we have quoted Marx in the *Manifesto,* "veiled by religious and political illusions"; but there are no illusions maintained with regard to the surplus product of labor itself.

In capitalist society, however, the situation is quite different. Whenever commodities come into play "the social character of men's labour appears to them as an objective character stamped upon the product of that labour."[19] This is, in fact, not so much the mysterious work *of* the commodity, but precisely what marks a useful object *as* a commodity. When individuals or groups of individuals produce, not simply for their own needs in the manner of Robinson Crusoe or an integrated communal society, but for one another, while only making "social contact" through the act of exchange of their products, when, that is to say, they make their particular labor a part of society as a whole's effort only via exchange, the "specific social character of each producer's labour does not show itself except in the act of exchange." But the act of exchange sets up a relationship not between the producers in any direct sense; the direct relationship it sets up is rather one between the products. Social relationships of production are thus mediated by a relationship between things. They appear to the producer in fact to *be* relationships between things.

It is this veil which hangs over social relations or, to use Marx's own famous metaphor, this "fetishism which attaches itself to the products of labour" in the form of commodities, which disguises the nature and existence of surplus in capitalist society. As he describes the capitalist system in reality as opposed to appearance in the third volume of *Capital:*[20]

Capital is not a thing, but rather a definite social production relation, belonging to a definite historical formation of society, which is manifested in a thing and lends this thing a specific social character. Capital is not the sum of the material and produced means of production. Capital is rather the means of production transformed into capital, which in themselves are no more capital than gold or silver in itself is money. It is the means of production monopolised by a certain section of society, confronting living labour-power as products and working conditions rendered independent of this very labour-power. . . .

Capital, that is to say, is not, as a dictionary might have it, "an accumulation of goods used for the production of more goods rather than for direct satisfaction of needs"; this is its appearance only. In reality it is power, derived from control of such goods and expressed through them, a power over surplus which constitutes a power over production and distribution which is ultimately a social power; the goods in question themselves, *as goods,* endure quite nicely, once produced, quite apart from any particular social power relations.

The bourgeois classical economists hence, though in their analysis of capitalism they came close to penetrating the veil of commodities to discover the social reality which lay behind it, never could do so. Although the labor theory of value was developed by them, they had, as bourgeois theorists, ultimately to remain in the realm of appearance, unable to follow it to its full conclusions; for it is in this realm of appearance that the bourgeois viewpoint and the ideology which flows from it find their basis. Laborers, freed from all traditional relationships of servitude, cannot *appear* to be giving over surplus to the masters of capital; nor can their labor appear to be forced; they must *seem* to be free agents coequal with other free agents, employer and employee, free and equal citizens all. In order to maintain these appearances they must enter into contracts in which they exchange equally with the employer. And in the reified realm of appearance they do; labour-power does, as we have seen, exchange at its value. There is a truth to this, despite its superficiality, just as it is true that our world appears geocentric, despite the discoveries of Copernicus; it is this truth concerning the realm of everyday appearance, which looks the same to capitalist and proletarian alike, from which bourgeois ideology grows; to operate in the realm of appearance is a necessary precondition of bourgeois ideology; and bourgeois theorists are for Marx forced to remain in this realm, inevitably blind to the reality which underlies it.

This is, it should be noted, the sense in which Marx's book presents, as its subtitle states, a *critique* of political economy rather than an economic theory on a par with other theories of economics. In its inclusion of economic theory within a broader theory of social development in bourgeois society, Marx finds its initial plausibility; though the test of a science is ultimately empirical, the plausibility of its first principles and its claim to uncover the reality behind appearance are at least formal requirements for good science on Marx's view.[21] That economic relations should be understandable in social terms is for him a sound beginning and a vast improvement on the old material-ism to which bourgeois political economy, with its inevitable confusion of social relations with things, was prone.[22] Economic laws are from this new standpoint to be seen, not as simple mechanistic relations between things, but as tendencies set in the context of a social dialectic of class struggle.

The importance and extent of the claim Marx is making in his attempt to demystify the fetishistic character of com-modities needs, I feel, even further elaboration; for our initial account—as also Marx's own account which it summarizes—of abstract labor and value has tended to obscure it somewhat. Granted that the product which he makes must have social utility, a producer in commodity production can still only reap benefits from the labor he expended to produce it, and satisfy his wants, if his product can be exchanged for others, that is, to pass from the language of the realm of appearance to that of reality, if "the mutual exchangeability of all kinds of useful private labour is an established social fact, and therefore the private useful labour of each producer ranks on an equality with that of all others."[23] This necessitates the positing of a common quality, value, which all useful products of labor are to have. The "positing" in question is, of course, not some theoretical act; it is the act of exchange, which, as we have already seen, is the act which makes social the labor of the commodity producer. It is not the case then that "abstract labor" is value in the sense that it is something which we can discover in the products of labor and conveniently use for the purpose of representing the socializing quality called value. "Quite the contrary," says Marx, "whenever, by an exchange, we equate as values our different products, by that very act, we also equate, as human labour, the different kinds of labour expended upon them." He adds that, though "we are not aware of this, nevertheless we do it."

The superficiality of Marx's proof that labor is the only thing which can be equated in equating commodities, to which we referred earlier, is thus seen to lie in its failure to touch upon the further question of *why* labor alone can assume this role. The answer to this question, we can now see, is—not that such a role falls to it by default—but that labor—in abstraction—is equated because exchange is a social process carried on ultimately between specialized producers whose problem is to find a means of socializing their "useful private labour" in order to make it a source of personal benefit for them. Given, as it is in the capitalist social form, that exchange alone is the only means available to do this, exchange must be bent to this service of socializing labor; the act of exchange is the act of socialization of the many specialized kinds of labor involved; hence it itself makes the equation between them.[24] The sense in which what we are used to calling economic relations are explained in terms of social relations in Marx is very strong indeed.

II *The Value/Price Transformation "Problem"*

In the first volume of *Capital*, where the process of production alone concerned Marx and interactions between the various spheres of capitalist production were largely ignored, he could without encountering difficulties treat the exchange value and prices of individual commodities as equivalent;[25] commodities sold at their values; exchange value, one easily assumed, was price. This assumption, however, which is that of the material in *Capital* as we have so far developed it, gives us only a picture of the general workings of capitalism, highlighting many of its essential features; it is an idealization which fails to capture all of the surface phenomena, the economic data of capitalism as it actually exists. Thus, in the third volume of *Capital*, when Marx sets out to correct the idealizations of Volume I, it quickly becomes apparent that the assumption is not correct; the prices of individual commodities do not in general equal their values. In order to see why this is so, it is necessary to introduce a few new concepts into our discussion.

It will also be convenient to express them in equations and employ some simple algebra.

The rate of profit or rate of return on an investment is of utmost importance in capitalism as it determines both where capital will be invested and possible rates of capital's growth. In Marx's system, in its essential form, it is expressed by the ratio of surplus value, that is, the value of unpaid labor, which we have already seen is profit, to the total capital laid out by the capitalist. If we call this rate P, the surplus value s, and divide the capital outlay into its two constituents, expenses for raw materials and machinery, which we will call c, and expenses for living labor-power (that is, the wages of the laborers who work with these), which we will call v, then[26]

$$(1) \qquad\qquad P = \frac{s}{c+v}$$

A second concept which we will need is that of the "organic composition of capital" which Marx defines as "the value-composition of capital, inasmuch as it is determined by and reflects its technical composition";[27] it is, that is to say, the ratio of constant capital invested, which basically represents capital in machinery—since raw materials are, roughly speaking, a fixed factor in production—to the input of living labor; as such it is a good indicator of the technical sophistication of an industry. If we let O stand for the organic composition and remember that labor input equals wages *plus* surplus, we have

$$(2) \qquad\qquad O = \frac{c}{s+v}$$

Finally, it will be helpful, though not here essential as is the case with the other two concepts, to introduce the notion of the "rate of surplus-value," the ratio of surplus value to value expended for labor-power, i.e., that of unpaid to paid labor or profit to wages.[28] If we call this s', then

$$(3) \qquad\qquad s' = \frac{s}{v}$$

Noting that $s = s'v$ and $c = O(s + v)$ or $O(s'v + v)$ we can write

$$P = \frac{s'v}{O(s'v + v) + v}$$

Factoring and dividing we find that

$$(4) \qquad P = \frac{s'}{O(s' + 1) + 1}$$

From this we can easily see that, if two spheres of production have equal rates of surplus value but different organic compositions, the sphere with a higher organic composition will have a lower rate of return on investment. Thus the oil industry, with almost fully automated refineries, having a high organic composition, would tend to deliver a lower return on investment than say, the automobile industry with a—relatively speaking— low organic composition.

However, notes Marx, "aside from unessential, incidental and mutually compensating distinctions, differences in the average rate of profit in the various branches of industry do not exist in reality, and could not exist without abolishing the entire system of capitalist production."[29] For, if, to continue with our above rather bizarre example, oil, over any considerable length of time, failed to give a return roughly equal to that of the automobile industry, capital would *en masse* migrate from it to autos and we would eventually arrive at a point where we had too many automobiles and nothing to put into their fuel tanks. In reality, of course, as Marx acknowledges, this would not happen. How are we then to account for this fact without giving up the view that value alone determines the movements of the capitalist system—that is, that the social relations in which we have so far anchored capitalist economics are its only determinants?

The answer which Marx gives is that the different rates of profit in the various branches of industry are reduced through the action of competition to a general rate of profit which is the weighted average of the different rates, each branch receiving its share of profit according to its share of the capital in all

branches. In other words, the movement of capital from spheres
with low profit rates to those with higher ones, flooding the
higher ones with investment out of proportion to the demand
for their goods, soon "creates such a ratio of supply to demand
that the average profit in the various spheres of production becomes the same."[30] This process is made possible by the fact
that the cost of producing an item, what Marx calls its "cost-
price," is—unlike the rate of profit—independent of the organic
composition of capital. "A commodity for whose production he
[the capitalist] must advance £100 costs him just as much
whether he invests $90_c + 10_v$, or $10_c + 90_v$. It costs him £100
in either case—no more and no less."[31] Thus, once competition
has established the average profit rate, profit can be added to
cost-price to give what Marx calls the "price of production"
of a commodity;[32] this will differ in general from its value—
the exception being found in those industries, if any, where
the value-computed profit rate (given in equations [1] and [4])
happens to equal the average. However, *in society as a whole*,
for society's total product, the summed prices of production of all
commodities will equal the sum of their values. For the redistribution of profit that goes on in the averaging process in
no way creates new profit—it merely redistributes what was
already there. And, since what was already there was the
surplus produced in the sum total of industries, the total profits
in society, the sum of the profits in all branches of production,
will—unlike profits in individual branches—equal the sum of
the surplus values produced.

It is as if, as previously noted, in the first volume of *Capital*
Marx were—with respect to this question—looking at capitalist
society as a whole as equivalent to one branch of industry.
We now see, however, that the branch which he there studies
is one which behaves exactly like that whose value-based rate
of profit happens to equal the average profit rate. In this way,
since society as a whole mirrors this sphere, he is in fact studying the relations of capitalist society as a whole in its most
general terms, at a greater level of abstraction than in Volume
III, but nonetheless as it is in certain essential features. It is
an idealization then, as I have previously described it, only
insofar as it fails to reveal the "fine-structure" features explored

in Volume III, not in that it represents no real features of the world.[33]

A feature, however, which it fails, at least in itself, to comprehend but which is implicit in the analysis above from the third volume is the fact that the averaging of profit rate, which we find in reality, gives the capitalist class a firm basis for unity in its struggle with labor. For, since the rate of profit is now seen to be clearly socially determined, the general rate of surplus value, that is, the rate of exploitation of labor in society generally, is equally valuable to all capitalists. As Marx puts it:[34]

In each particular sphere of production the individual capitalist, as well as the capitalists as a whole, take direct part in the exploitation of the total working-class by the totality of capital and in the degree of that exploitation, not only out of general class sympathy, but also for direct economic reasons. For assuming all other conditions . . . to be given, the average rate of profit depends on the intensity of exploitation of the sum total of labour by the sum total of capital.

A glance at equation (4) will confirm this, the rate of surplus value, s', being this measure of intensity of exploitation, and the equation, as explained above, holding good for society as a whole.

Such society-wide movements of capital, and, in consequence, labor, are Marx's chief interest in *Capital;* it is the system as a whole which the book ultimately aims at explaining. This is in keeping with his view that political developments, which he characterizes as class-wide confrontations, are the truly significant events in the working class' progress toward the seizure of power.[35] His interest in economic theory, reflecting his political aims for the workers, centers around broad economic movements, because he believes that such broad movements ultimately condition political developments; as capital finds its class unity via total social capital so also does labor in its increasingly unified resistance to it.

Before proceeding to other topics in *Capital* we should note that Marx's solution to the problem raised by the existence of a general rate of profit has not proved acceptable to quite a few theorists, including some who are for the most part highly sympathetic to his views. Among his bourgeois enemies it has been, moreover, a traditional rallying point for criticism, most believing that it cannot be "corrected" while leaving the labor theory of value intact. It is undoubtedly the most controversial theoretical issue in Marxism, and hence worthy of more than our passing attention. In the remainder of this section, I will therefore detail the criticism in an attempt to show how it misunderstands what Marx, in *Capital*, is trying to do.

The objection of all of the critics is for the most part the same. It was raised initially by Eugene Böhm-Bawerk shortly after Engels's publication of Volume III.[36] Paul Sweezy, a Marxist economist who accepts the criticism, presents it, together with the Ricardian economist, Ladislaus von Bortkiewicz's alternative "solution," as follows.[37] Suppose that we divide industry into three branches. Department I produces only means of production, that is, raw materials and machinery to be used in production; Department II produces goods which the workers consume; and Department III produces goods for capitalists, that is, luxury goods. Assume what Marx calls a condition of "simple reproduction," that is, an economy in which capitalists annually spend all of their surplus and replace all constant capital used, and workers spend all of their wages. Such a static system does not, of course, exist anywhere in reality nor, as we will see, could it; but, says Sweezy, "going from value calculation to price calculation has no connection with the question whether the economic system as a whole is stationary or expanding"; the model, though an idealization, will do.

Applying Marx's method of averaging to the situation illustrated in the below table for the three capitals, each with a different organic composition, we find that the following figures obtain:

Department	Constant Capital c	Variable Capital v	Surplus Value s	Value $c+v+s$	Profit	Price of Production
I	250	75	75	400	108⅓	433⅓
II	50	75	75	200	41⅔	166⅔
III	100	50	50	200	50	200
Totals	400	200	200	800	200	800

Everything in the table at first looks in order. The average rate of profit is

$$P = \frac{s}{c + v} = \frac{200}{600} = 33\tfrac{1}{3}\%$$

The total profit equals the total surplus value, both being 200, and total value equals the total of the prices of production, 800 for each. Also, in *value* terms, the condition of simple reproduction obtains: total surplus equals total value in Department III—the capitalists use up all surplus on their luxuries; total constant capital used in production equals total value produced in Department I—all constant capital used is replaced; and total variable capital equals the total value produced in Department II—the workers spend their entire wages. However, when we look at prices of production, it appears that the conditions of equilibrium for simple reproduction have, in the transformation from value terms, broken down. The total constant capital used is 400 while the total of prices of production in Department I is 433⅓, and the total variable capital is 200 while the total prices of production in Department II is only 166⅔. Surplus does equal the Department III output, but this is "a mere accident of the way the table has been constructed," notes Sweezy. "Only one conclusion is possible, namely, that the Marxian method of transformation is logically unsatisfactory." For no one would want to hold that the mere "mechanics of transforming values into prices" could cause such disturbances. The problem lies, he adds, in the fact that in Marx's scheme the constant and variable capital used up in production—that is, the cost-price—is "expressed in value terms" while outputs are "expressed in price terms." Marx has only gone "half way in transforming values into prices."[38]

From here Sweezy proceeds to offer Bortkiewicz's "correction" of Marx which he finds—although Bortkiewicz himself seems not to have found it—compatible with Marx's general views. The alternative solution is itself problematic as are other alternatives produced since.[39] Rather than deal here with it and the others, many of which are mathematically fairly sophisticated, I shall look briefly instead at the above "problem"; for it is somewhat doubtful that Marx's "error" is actual, the construction of the so-called "problem" being beset by a number of confusions in itself.

We should note at the outset that, since the equilibrium conditions for total surplus value and profit, as well as values and prices of production hold, the difficulty is not located in the description of the functioning of the system as a whole; those economic considerations which are Marx's chief concern, namely, system-wide movements, will be left intact if we can adequately explain the apparent disruption of the conditions of simple reproduction in the Sweezy example. This, it turns out, is not that difficult to do. The simple reproduction schema were used by Marx only in very different contexts than they are in it;[40] he himself, in his own example, uses five branches of industry which are, for the purposes of the example, unrelated; such possible interrelationships as exist between Departments I, II, and III are, that is to say, ignored by Marx. This is not, however, an oversight on his part. He ignores them quite consciously in order to avoid complications in his presentation which are unnecessary for his purposes in it. For the introduction of relationships of this sort will invariably result in just the sort of "errors" that appear in Sweezy's example. When capitalists from Departments II and III, the wage and luxury goods departments, buy machinery or raw materials from Department I, they will pay a price which has, due to the Marxian averaging process, a price of production for its basis. When, on the other hand, they make use of this constant capital, it is value—and not price of production—which is transferred to their product. Consequently, we have in such schemas as Sweezy's a mixing of the two, values proper and their converted forms, prices of production, which will, of course, lead to confusions. As Marx himself puts it:[41]

Since the price of production may differ from the value of a commodity, it follows that the cost-price of a commodity containing this price of production of another commodity may also stand above or below that portion of its total value derived from the value of the means of production consumed by it. . . . there is always the possibility of an error if the cost-price of a commodity . . . is identified with the value of the means of production consumed by it.

For Sweezy this is the hub of the problem, the deep reason why Marx's analysis only goes "half-way." For Marx, however, the analysis "does not necessitate a closer examination of this point."

The question now becomes, Why, if Marx was himself aware of the possibility of "error," did he—in so cavalier a manner—brush aside the bugbear of post-Marx Marxian theory? The answer seems to be that he was not trying to solve the problem which his critics believe he is. He is not, that is to say, formulating a theory of price. Prices of production are not, first of all, phenomenal market prices anyway; nor does he ever wrongly identify them as such. They are closer to the phenomenal level of observable market prices than are values because they take into account the process of formation of a general rate of profit; but they are not prices in this sense.[42] What Marx *is* doing—his critics to the contrary—is studying the process of movement of the total system. And, for the total system, as David Yaffe observes:[43]

That the cost price of a commodity produced by an individual capital is not equal to the value of the commodities consumed in its production does not alter the basic point. We have to regard the individual capital as part of the total social capital, and for the total capital they coincide. . . . For total social capital . . . the total cost price is equal to the total value consumed [just as] total value is equal to total price and total surplus value is equal to total profit. The movement of individual capitals . . . does not, and cannot, change this.

It is thus, continues Yaffe, from this viewpoint beside the point to worry about conversions of "inputs" (constant and variable capital) from values to prices of production as Sweezy and the other critics do. Since the movement of individual capitals only serves to redistribute the surplus or profit in the system as a whole, "the constant capital and variable capital [the "inputs"] therefore represent the actual capitals invested in the different spheres of production as shares of the total capital, and as such remain unchanged in the transformation process." The process of averaging, that is to say, effects the individual surplus values only and leaves the values of input capitals intact in each sphere irrespective of discrepancies in cost-prices; values invested and consumed in relation to total value are one thing and actual cost-prices and prices of production formed by the process of social averaging quite another.

We have seen here then the depth of Marx's concentration on the total, overall process of capitalism, a fact which eludes his critics, both friendly and hostile. Such concentration, of course, leaves him without a theory of prices, much to the critics' dismay. However, this lack is negligible from the standpoint of the task he has set himself—to uncover the developing social relations which underlie the interactions, both social and economic, which we observe in the daily functioning of capitalist society. Also, it is worth remembering, lest we lose perspective on this matter, that Marx is not alone in failing to provide us with a theory of price; no theory to date does so fully adequately—including the much-touted marginal-utility approach.

III *Labor and the Accumulation of Capital*

Capitalism, as we have already noted, never in reality can limit itself to the simple reproduction of the economy as it stands; of necessity, a process of accumulation and growth characterizes the system. The capitalist who consumed all his profits—save those necessary merely to keep his operation moving along as usual—would hardly find himself prestigious in a system where "only as personified capital is the capitalist respectable."[44] It is accumulation and subsequent reinvestment alone which allows him to extend his influence. In fact, given the tendency of the system to develop, accumulation is necessary for a given capitalist even to maintain the influence he has. This tendency is, of course, in part to be understood as resulting from competition among capitalists to secure the power accompanying an increase in capital; and, insofar as it is, we might put the matter more simply by saying that competition for power and prestige in capitalist circles forces the individual capitalist to accumulate and reinvest—quite apart from his personal desires for increased influence—if he wants to take the part of capitalist in the system at all. However, competition among capitalists is not the only factor which leads to the development of industry and wealth under capitalism. Once the initial process of accumulation through competition has begun, labor too exerts a pressure which forces the system to expand.

Since accumulation is ultimately nothing more than an amassing of labor-time, the rate of accumulation will—if the number of laborers remains relatively stable—find "a check in the natural limits of the exploitable labouring population";[45] if, moreover, "the requirements of accumulation begin to surpass the customary supply of labour . . . a rise of wages takes place."[46] Such a rise, if left unchecked, could easily eat away the surplus that allows accumulation, and even that portion which goes for maintenance and the capitalists' revenue; under such conditions, therefore, a free market economy is impossible and wages must be regulated by force. This was in fact the practice, as we have seen in Chapter 2, during the early days of capitalism when these conditions by and large held. After the industrial revolution, however, the introduction of labor-saving machinery provided a mechanism for producing a relative surplus population which made such wage-control legislation obsolete. Whenever wages in a given industry began to rise due to an undersupply of laborers, machinery was introduced in the industry "and in a moment the labourers were redundant again."[47] The Malthusians might spout all the nonsense they cared to about natural tendencies toward absolute overpopulation; the "overpopulation" which provides industrial capital with its "reserve army of labor" is a product of the system itself, and quite independent of whether or not the population of potential laborers grows absolutely.

The size of this reserve army, it will be noted, determines the general fluctuation of wages. When industry expands, the army contracts and wages rise until they infringe on the capitalists' surplus; thereupon, the rate of accumulation and expansion slows, laborers are laid off, swelling the reserve army's ranks once more, and causing a fall in wages. Running parallel to this process of wage fluctuation is, of course, that of the periodic business cycle as the rate of accumulation effects and is effected by the periodically expanding and contracting reserve army. Not only will the size of the reserve army vary periodically, however; it will also steadily climb in its numbers as industry continues to grow. For with the growth of industry the process of accumulation for reinvestment does not in general maintain a steady ratio between capital invested in labor and capital invested in machinery; it favors rather machinery, so that growth in the demand for labor does not keep pace with the accumulation of capital.

This fact has led Marx in both the first volume of *Capital* and his simultaneously composed address before the International's General Council to maintain that "the general tendency of capitalistic production is...to sink the average standard of wages, [that is]...to push the *value of labour* more or less to its *minimum limit*."[48] It will, that is to say, tend—as time and accumulation progresses—to undermine the "traditional" standard of living already in existence in a given laboring population and move them always closer to the physical minimum needed to live and work as "a quick succession of unhealthy and short-lived generations." Ironically, as Marx puts it in *Capital*, "the higher the productiveness of labour, the greater is the pressure of the labourers on the means of employment, the more precarious, therefore,...their condition of existence."[49] The price of labor must tend to fall absolutely to a bare subsistence level as its supply steadily grows. Trade unions, in their day to day economic struggles, can retard such a tendency but not, he notes in his address to the General Council (that is, in *Value, Price and Profit*), change its direction. The progress of modern industry must "progressively turn the scale in favour of the capitalist against the working man."[50]

Marx's critics have attacked him for his adherence to this doctrine of the so-called "progressive emiseration of labour" more severely than for any other of his views—with the possible exception of the supposed value/price transformation problem that we examined above.[51] For many in fact it is thought to provide grounds for a total rejection of Marxist theory. For, if the theory predicts such a downward secular trend in living standards, they argue, the fact that, by and large, standards of living have risen in the industrial nations from Marx's day to our own disconfirms the theory. Granted the above antecedent, this would seem to be true; at the very least, at any rate, such an anomaly would require some drastic revisions in Marx's work. Two questions, however, bear careful examination before we accept these conclusions. First, is Marx in the works cited actually predicting such a downward trend? Second, if he is, does such a prediction spring really from the very foundations of the theory of *Capital?*—or is it rather a prediction based on one of several possible readings of the theory, which, as we have seen in the chapter on methodology, is far from straightforwardly deterministic in its form?

Looking at the former question first, it seems safe to say that—though there are certainly several passages both in *Capital* and elsewhere in Marx's writings where he might easily be read as making such a prediction—there is also room in all of these to interpret him differently. To best see this possible alternative interpretation, let us turn back to the passages from *Value, Price and Profit* where he addresses the issue most directly.

The claim he makes here is that a "general tendency" toward the impoverishment of labor is present in capitalist accumulation. In a dialectical setting, where tendencies of necessity call forth countertendencies, the first thing to be noted is that a tendency toward poverty in no way guarantees that poverty will result. The class struggle ultimately will decide the outcome of any such opposition of tendencies and the results of this struggle cannot, on Marx's view, be gleaned from any mechanistic account of events.[52] Still, Marx *does* claim that day to day economic struggles, the "unavoidable guerilla fights incessantly springing up from the never-ceasing encroachments of capital," can only retard the tendency, since capital's power increases in direct proportion to its ever enlarging wealth. The tendency toward impoverishment outweighs, it seems, the counterinfluence of economic struggle. From this claim Marx's critics have concluded that Marx believes that the workers' living standard must decrease. In reality, however, he is in no way driven to such a conclusion. For it is only isolated *economic* actions which he claims provide no adequate counterinfluence to the tendency toward impoverishment. He at no point states that *political*—that is, class-wide—countermeasures cannot begin to reverse this trend. The emphasis in his speech, as always, is in fact on the need for political action, though his focus on organization for the *ultimate* political act, the revolutionary seizure of political power, tends to obscure this *general* point.

Viewed in this way, Marx's claims begin to look more reasonable. The decisive factors in labor's struggle which have allowed its living standard to increase rather than decrease over the past century have in fact *been* political actions. It is welfare benefits, minimum wage laws, unemployment insurance, the union shop, child labor laws, and similar measures—all won on a class-wide political basis—which have insured whatever power labor holds today.[53] Had labor contented itself with isolated economic actions alone, it is very likely that a tendency toward impoverishment might be what we would see.[54] To leave the matter here, however, would be to fail to distinguish Marx's view from the liberal reformism which, as often as not, sponsored the political measures mentioned above. For revolution is not for him a program grafted onto less radical political action but its organically necessary outgrowth and ultimately necessary end. Each political victory of the working class puts a stress on the system which calls forth countermeasures by a capitalist class whose potential *economic* lordship over labor is steadily growing.[55] Increasingly, political compromise becomes more difficult to achieve. The working class, in such a situation, must finally take power or lose most or all the political gains it has made. This, of course, is a far more controversial claim than that which merely equates working class power with political action per se. Its evaluation I defer to the closing section of the book.

We have seen then that Marx may well have never held increasing impoverishment to be inevitable. Our interpretation of his viewpoint, moreover, whether or not it seems ultimately reasonable to say it was Marx's, gives an automatic answer to our second question—namely, Is a falling real wage a necessary consequence of Marx's general theory? For if the interpretation is not inconsistent with the theory—and I see no reason to believe that it is—the answer is a clear "no." A coherent alternative to progressive impoverishment which is consistent with the general theory of *Capital* is possible in that we have above presented one. Marx was involved in political estimations and not theoretical deductions in whatever speculations he might be thought to have made concerning the future wages of labor; his theory in itself does not determine this point.

IV   *The Fundamental Contradiction of Capitalism as Expressed in the Tendency of the Profit Rate to Fall*

The above account of "tendencies" toward emiseration has begun to give us some notion of the role of dialectics in *Capital*. To see it in its full generality, however, we must return for the moment to that most basic form of the capitalist system, the commodity. A commodity, as we have seen, embodies of necessity two kinds of value—use value and exchange value—the former being presupposed if the latter is to be set at all; use value is, moreover, a relation which exists only between an object and its potential user while exchange value is in reality a social relation. As such, these two kinds of value are not—locked together as they are in objects via the commodity form of capitalism—simple parallel properties, united only as two distinct and unrelated aspects of a single essence; on the contrary, as the capitalist system develops, they prove to be, not only related, but incompatible properties through which the human relations embodied in them come into dialectical conflict or "contradiction."

The methods of production which capitalism employs are, of course, methods for the production of *use values*, just as the commodities which are produced must embody use value. Increased production via an increasing productivity of labor, therefore, represents an increase in use value; with increased productivity the amount of use values available to a society grows. The social relations of production of capitalism, on the other hand—those relations for which *exchange value* provides expression—deal with increased productivity and production only insofar as they bear on the wage and the growth of capital, the social product measured in terms of *exchange value;* for the product in its money expression is all that these relations know. In the tendency toward impoverishment of the working class—that is, the diminution of their enjoyment of use values—as capital accumulates, we have already seen the contradiction between use value and exchange value at play. This contradiction, we can now also observe, is the capitalist-specific version of the general contradiction between the methods or means of production and the relations of production, a contradiction which, as

148

we have previously seen, leads, on Marx's view, to the super-cession of the social form which embodies it.

The forms which the basic contradiction of capitalism may take are many. Central to most, if not all, of these is, however, the conflict between the tendency of the profit rate to fall in a developing industrial capitalism and the factors which counter-act this tendency. To see why the tendency exists, consider again equation (4) above in which the profit rate P is expressed as a function of s', the rate of surplus value, and O, the organic composition of capital:

$$(4) \qquad P = \frac{s'}{O(s' + 1) + 1}$$

Remembering here that O in general expresses the level of technological sophistication of the system and hence the level of productivity insofar as this has been developed through the introduction of machinery, we see that—holding s' constant—the more sophisticated the system, that is, the more it employs machinery and the higher its consequent social productivity, the lower is the return on an investment. The rate of profit will fall even as—due to this higher productivity—both profit or capital and the mass of use values, which represents real social wealth, increase.

It will fall as these grow, however, only insofar as "counter-acting influences" inherent in the system fail to retard or check its fall. Marx lists the following as the six "most general [of these] counterbalancing forces":[56] (1) the possibility of increas-ing s', the ratio of surplus labor-time to that kept by the worker in the form of wages; for, although s' appears in the denominator as well as the numerator of P expressed as a function of s' and O in equation (4), an inspection of the equation will reveal that, as s' increases, P will as well; (2) the possibility of de-pressing wages below the value of labor-power; (3) the cheap-ening of elements of constant capital with its consequent deval-uation of the organic composition O; (4) the "freeing up" of labor for new industries with a low organic composition, the profit rate from which, being averaged into the general rate of profit, will tend to raise it; (5) the encouragement of foreign trade and imperialism in order to cheapen both the raw materials portion of constant capital—in the manner of (3) above—and, via cheap imported necessities, the value of labor-power itself; (6) the sale of stock to raise capital, a process which obscures the real profit rate, making it appear higher than it is to potential investors.

All of the above, it should be noted, are factors which encourage the growth of capital; they all, at the same time, however, either presuppose or encourage *and* ultimately both presuppose and encourage the same tendency toward increased productivity which causes the profit rate to fall. The simplest way to increase s' is, of course, to lengthen the working day; but, as this method has both its natural limits and, as labor organizes, still further *imposed* limits, the only recourse left to capital is intensification of labor during the relatively fixed working day, a process which tends to introduce still more machinery into the system, ultimately exacerbating the problem it is designed to solve. To some extent again constant capital can be cheapened by careful use of by-products and other capital-saving methods; but such measures are relatively limited in scope. A more important factor, which does in fact automatically cheapen constant capital, is the depreciation of already existing capital as new methods replace those which were used in its production;[57] but, once again, these new methods are generally the very ones which lead to an increase in the mass of constant capital employed and hence a falling profit rate. The reserve army of labor on which the possibility of both the second and fourth counterbalancing forces is based is likewise, as we saw in the previous section, dependent for its existence on increasing productivity, as is also usually an increase in foreign trade; turning to stock capital, finally, we see that its existence presupposes large-scale enterprises based on this very same factor, and that it furthermore encourages their continued growth.

We find then that increased productivity (the use value or means of production side of the fundamental contradiction of capitalism) both produces and is produced by its negation in the above factors which lead to the growth of capital (the exchange value or relations of production side) while at the same time—via the tendency of the profit rate to fall—it wars against it. "The means," writes Marx, "unconditional development of

the productive forces of society—comes continually into conflict with the limited purpose [of capitalism], the self-expansion
of existing capital. The capitalist mode of production is, for this
reason, a historical means of developing the material forces
of production and ... at the same time a continual conflict
between this its historical task and its own corresponding
relations of social production."[58] Moreover, since the warring
forces have the above-described intimate relationship, as the
conflict continues, it must of necessity intensify. For each move
to check the falling profit rate is, as we have seen, ultimately a
move which will encourage it once more as well, and each time
on a grander scale. Intensified labor, expanded trade, new industries, a growing reserve army, stock companies—all are
measures which in one way or another involve a growth in
the constant capital employed.

Are we thus to assume that—despite the setbacks of counter-
influences—we should see a gradual fall in the profit rate over
time? Is this the expression of the above intensification which
we should expect to observe? Many interpreters of the theory
have thought so. Marx himself, however, seems ambivalent on
the point. With respect to the rate of surplus value—the ultimately crucial factor as our account below will show—he *does*
say at one point in his discussion that its increase has "certain
insurmountable limits" as a counterinfluence which allow it to
"check the fall in the rate of profit" but not to "prevent it altogether."[59] He seems nevertheless to discount the somewhat
dubious reasons he gives for so rigidly holding to this view,
in an earlier general statement where he simply says that, the
law being a mere tendency, "it is only *under certain circumstances* and only after long periods that its effects become
strikingly pronounced."[60]

Milton Fisk, in his brilliant little essay, "Rate of Profit and
Class Struggle," to which we have alluded earlier, makes explicit what these circumstances are in the course of demonstrating
that a search for confirmation of the law via an empirical observation of a falling profit rate is a wrongheaded approach.[61]
The rate of profit in a well-developed industrial capitalism will
fall, observes Fisk, if and only if either of the two following
conditions are met:

(1) A proportional increase in the level of productivity of labor is matched or outstripped by a similar increase in the value tied-up in constant capital as measured by the organic composition, O;

(2) A productivity increase outstrips a similar change in the degree of exploitation as measured by the rate of surplus value, s'.

Productivity here is understood as net productivity—the total socially necessary labor-time that is involved in the production of an item at any time t as compared to that involved in its production at some earlier time t_0.

Since O in fact need not grow, *of necessity*, at as fast a rate as productivity and, since s'—despite labor's opposition—might indeed increase even faster than productivity, we are not insured that the profit rate will fall. What we are insured of, however, is that the class struggle will determine whether it does at any given time. For the second condition is met only when labor resists increased exploitation while, at the same time, either it or intracapitalist rivalry calls forth a need for increased productivity, in a manner which capitalism cannot resist. The first condition likewise is met in general under similar circumstances. For, although the use of capital-saving devices to reduce O as productivity increases has—as we have noted—some limited use, O will, in the last analysis, be reduced through cheapening the production of constant capital, a process which will usually involve the need to increase the degree of exploitation of labor, hence, making a resistance to this increased exploitation an occasion for the fulfillment of condition (2).[62]

The intensification we can therefore expect over time as a result of the dialectical interplay which centers around a falling rate of profit is an intensification of the class struggle. As Fisk puts it, "Inflation, speed-up, tax increases and unemployment are the sort of things that would confirm the law."[63] As time goes on, moreover, the problems resulting from these will become more severe, as the capitalist class, seeking to encourage capital's growth or "self-expansion," encounters "a growing difficulty in insuring the necessary discipline on the part of labor and in finding the necessary available capital in order to prevent the dominance of the side of the contradiction represented by Marx's law."[64] The confirmation of the law of the tendency for the profit rate to fall is thus found in socioeconomic and political phenomena rather than in an isolated economic fact. Remembering that economic phenomena are for Marx but expressions of these anyway, this should prove no great surprise.

Do, however, the social and political facts of the last hundred years tend to confirm the prediction? Fisk believes that they do. From the best available data we have for the United States we can, first of all, conclude that s' has tended to increase over this time. This fact becomes quite striking when we observe that, during the same period, labor has in general made significant gains in its standard of living. Capital, while willing to give in on this score during boom periods, has nonetheless, it seems, consistently resisted the "workers' efforts to reduce the length of the work day, to put an end to speed up, and to increase their share [that is, their proportional share] of the growing surplus."[65] It has, moreover, during the twentieth century exhibited a need for inflation which—except during crisis periods—has been a steady secular trend. This inflation, which is encouraged by the growth of economic oligopolies and monopolies in this century, provides a means for depressing wages below the currently accepted value of labor-power which is far more subtle and difficult to resist than are wage cuts, which are always flagrantly visible. During crisis periods, however, these and layoffs can also be easily effected to the same end. Crisis itself in fact is often a response to the profit rate's tendency to fall, as funds for investment grow scarce with a lowering of the profit rate, causing recession and depression to follow a period of expansion. Finally, the permanent arms economy, which has been a familiar feature of the United States and several other capitalist economies for the last thirty-five years, readily lends itself to an explanation that presupposes this aspect of the Marxian dialectic. For, if we assume that the tendency toward a falling rate of profit, together with its capital expansive responses, is "the basis for a chronic capital shortage," we can see that "among the various ways the problem is alleviated is government subsidization of military industry and government purchase of military equipment."[66]

All of the above factors then—speed up, lack of increased leisure time, inflation, monopoly, and the arms economy—point to the truth of Marx's analysis here. In the conclusion to this work which follows, we will examine this question of confirmation or disconfirmation of Marx's theory in yet more general terms.

CHAPTER 7

Marx and the Contemporary World

OVER one hundred years have passed since the publication of the first volume of *Capital*. In that time, Marx's name and work have been bandied about in support of the ideology of numerous peasant revolutions; and yet to date there has been no successful socialist revolution in any of the advanced industrial nations of which he wrote. Surely capitalism has proved more resilient than Marx had anticipated it to be. Though this is not as devastating to his theory as many critics would like to make it appear, since the dialectic is, as we have seen, totally incapable of dating even approximately the revolutionary breaking point of a system, it does seem safe to say that not only the time elapsed with no revolutionary transformation of society but also the extent of the development of the productive forces under capitalism would probably have surprised Marx. There is, however, one place in his writings where he deals specifically with such an eventuality, showing himself fully cognizant of its theoretical possibility, whatever his political speculations might have been. I would like to deal here in closing with this extended passage, in part because it illuminates further some general aspects of Marx's thought, which have been distorted in its transformation into an ideology of the underdeveloped nations, but mainly because it seems to me highly relevant to understanding contemporary events and movements in the developed capitalist world.

The passage is found in the "Grundrisse" notebooks and concerns that general aspect of capitalism's fundamental contradiction which Marx here describes as the "contradiction between the foundation of bourgeois production (value as measure) and its development."[1] It is obvious that "to the degree that large industry develops, the creation of real wealth comes to

154

depend less on labour time and on the amount of labour employed than on the power of the agencies set in motion during
labour time"; it will come to be, that is to say, ultimately dependent upon "the general state of science and . . . the progress of
technology" to a far greater extent than it is upon labor-time.
As capitalism develops then "it presses to reduce labour time to
a minimum" and replace it with technology; and yet, through
exchange value, it continues to posit "labour time . . . as sole
measure and source of wealth." The contradiction is the developing system itself:

On the one side . . . it calls to life all the powers of science and of
nature . . . in order to make the creation of wealth independent
(relatively) of the labour time employed on it. On the other side, it
wants to use labour time as the measuring rod for the giant social
forces thereby created, and to confine them within the limits required
to maintain the already created value as value.

But ultimately such forces cannot be so confined: "As soon as
labour in the direct form has ceased to be the great wellspring of
wealth, labour time ceases and must cease to be its measure,
and hence exchange value [must cease to be the measure] of
use value." With this the conditions which lie at the foundations
of capitalism disappear.

If we consider for a moment a hypothetical limiting case, we
can see why this is so quite clearly. Imagine if you will a world
that is fully automated. Labor here is superfluous and with it
also the wage. Under such conditions it is easy to see that
either the machinery keeps churning out use values with no wage
earners to purchase them or the wageless unemployed use them
without the blessings of purchase. The former case is, of course,
an impossibility, since capital no longer has a market to provide
an incentive for production. The latter is an advanced stage of
communism. This limiting case will undoubtedly never be completely realized. Marx is probably correct in his assertion that,
even in a future society which consciously maximizes the leisure
which is the prerequisite for the "development of human
energy . . . [as] an end in itself," *some* necessary labor will always
be required.[2] Still, a social reality which approaches it closely

enough to render capitalism thoroughly obsolete is realizable—
probably even with the technology we have available to us
today. Capitalism is, "despite itself, instrumental in creating the
means of social disposable time, in order to reduce labour time
for the whole society to a diminishing minimum, and thus to
free everyone's time for their own development."[3] The fact that
it rather uses this "disposable time" for the creation of its
surplus lays the ground for a contradiction; and "the more this
contradiction develops, the more does it become evident that
the growth of the forces of production can no longer be bound
up with the appropriation of alien labour . . . that the mass of
workers must themselves appropriate their own surplus labour."
From a highly developed capitalism, a more advanced form of
communism than was possible in the late nineteenth and early
twentieth centuries should be expected to emerge.

How likely is it to do so, however, and what signs if any are
there that it exists in potential in the contemporary capitalist
world? To begin to try to answer these questions we should back
up a moment and look for expressions of the above described
contradiction in contemporary capitalism; for it is only in the
context of it that we can hope to discover that resistance to
capital's use of "disposable time" which we might be able to read
as potentially revolutionary in form. As the above wider contradiction includes that which centers around the tendency of
the profit rate to fall, we have in fact seen some of the expressions
of this contradiction already in Milton Fisk's analysis of the
tendency's current manifestations.[4] Three of these in particular
warrant closer examination; those which center around the
tendency toward monopoly in contemporary capitalism, the
problem of "speed-up" in production, and the stubborn con-
stancy of the average work week over the past thirty years.[5]

Monopoly is an expression of capital's desire to solve the contradiction in its most general form completely on its own terms.
It is, that is to say, an attempt within the framework of capitalism to drop labor-time as its "measuring rod," in that monopoly
pricing is, as we have seen, independent of labor as the basis of
exchange. In doing so, however, it both preys on the still competitive sectors of the economy and the wage workers, whose
real incomes diminish as prices are set irrespective of the cost

of the reproduction of labor-power. This latter fact in turn has repercussions even in monopoly (oligopoly) sectors whenever consumer goods are the items involved. The auto industry, thus, just as much as either labor or more competitive industries, resisted oil's price rises over recent years. Monopoly, moreover, as well as breeding resistance, also breeds further monopoly, each time exposing in greater nakedness the power relations on which capitalism is based.

"Speed-up," however, far more than monopoly, has met with labor's active resistance over the past several years. For here the level of organization necessary to resist is much lower, allowing expressions of resistance to be felt clearly even before a mature form of expression has been discovered by the class. The sabotage and wildcat walkouts of workers at the highly sophisticated General Motors' plant in Lordstown, Ohio provides perhaps its most striking instance; but it was one of many in the late 1960s and early 1970s both in the United States and abroad.

Coupled with this resistance, we find a new attitude toward work—especially among younger blue collar workers. If the companies won't provide increased leisure, the workers will take it for themselves, both by laying down on the job and by not showing up for work. In a recent article, Bennett Kremen, after documenting at firsthand on-the-job work resistance among young workers at United States Steel's Chicago Southworks, quotes the following statistics from a Ford executive:[6]

From 1957 to '61 ... we averaged 2.6 percent of our production workers off on a given day. Each year since then, the figure rose until it reached 5.8 percent in 1968. On Mondays and Fridays though, the figure often goes almost to 15 percent. And that really hurts inside those plants. Right now we're averaging 5.1 percent for the year.

A General Motors' official adds that "only 15 percent of the work force ... generates most of the late arrivals and absences ... most of these men [being] concentrated among the newer workers under 35." While a "clever old workingman" sums it up as follows for Kremen: "These kids have a different outlook on life. They've never been broke the way we were ... *they don't even know how to take the crap we took!*"

Even in relatively backward capitalist nations such an "outlook on life" seems to emerge easily today. In the recent abortive attempts to establish socialism in both Chile and Portugal, the concept has meant something far different to the militant younger workers than it does to the party bureaucrat. To the former it means shorter hours and a better life through higher wages; to the latter, state planning with a view to national development through increased productivity. In the nineteenth century, workers' interests and such planning were identical; in the late twentieth century, from the international perspective which seems to have captured these revolutionary movements, they appear to be opposed.

Work orientation disappears with the assembly line's final destruction of large-scale, socially significant, skilled blue collar labor.[7] Yet even antibureaucratic socialist intellectuals—being mainly highly skilled white collar professionals—tend to fail to see this and continue to propagate an ideology which centers around job control, a holistic engagement in production, and the romanticization of the laborer, totally disregarding that, for the blue collar worker, these are increasingly obsolete ideals.

The new "outlook" is nonetheless something which is not limited to blue collar labor; it manifests itself in all strata of the working class as one of the mainstays of the "counterculture movement." It is this more general movement in fact which has been largely responsible for the form that blue collar work resistance has taken. Still in its infancy, the expression of opposition to capitalism in the countercultural mode is often sentimental, communalistic in a Utopian manner, and burdened with a hatred of machines.[8] How it will develop and whether it can achieve political coherency and transcend its sentimentality is still difficult to say.[9] Already capital has launched its counter-offensive with its decision to accept an increasingly deep recession through the latter half of the 1970s, so that any form labor's movement against it takes for the present, will have to be in terms of this.

Marx never dealt systematically with the question of political organization nor was his own political practice especially enlightening in this matter; and Lenin, though valuable to study for both his successes *and* mistakes, can hardly in himself be thought to fill the gap.[10] The specter of communism has taken on an ectoplasmic fullness since it began haunting Europe's capitals in Marx's day. It remains for the working class to discover the political form which will make this now rich spirit manifest.

Notes and References

Chapter One

1. This dispute, as we will see, reflects an ambivalence in Hegel's own attitudes toward religion and politics, the orthodox interpretation gleaning most from his later works and the Young Hegelian's from the earlier.

2. The occasion for this intervention of the censors was a series of editorials criticizing the Russian government which drew complaints from the Russian embassy.

3. The manuscripts of 1844 were not published until 1932. They have led, since shortly after that time, to a political and theoretical controversy concerning their relationship to Marx's subsequent work which is discussed in detail in Chapter 5 of this book.

4. The culmination of this research was his book, *The Condition of the Working Class in England in 1844,* trans. Henderson and Chaloner (Palo Alto: Stanford Univ. Press, 1958).

5. *Manifesto of the Communist Party,* Sec. 1 (New York: International Publishers, 1971).

6. This is not to say that activist intellectuals were not found in such societies—at times they had even organized them; but their energy and even most of their leadership was provided by craftsmen who had educated themselves in philosophy and social thought.

7. Gracchus Babeuf, after the power of the tradesmen and workers was broken with the execution of Robespierre, attempted a conspiratorial *putsch* against the French Directory in 1796 in order to restore that power. The *putsch* failed and Babeuf was executed. His ideas, which he explained eloquently at his trial, were protosocialist.

8. Despite its inaccuracies the *Manifesto* is probably the best introduction to Marx's thought there is. The reader entirely unacquainted with Marxism is thus advised either to read the *Manifesto* itself at this point or turn to my summary of it in section one of the next chapter.

9. See *Neue Rheinische Zeitung Politisch-Ökonomische Revue,* nos. 5–6, (May–October, 1850).

10. Marx himself says "three," combining our Volumes 2 and 3 into one.

11. The fact that it is written for an "intelligent working man" should not be construed as implying that the work is designed as propaganda. It was rather felt by Marx to be necessary to compose it in such a way in order that it be useful to leaders and strategists who had and would emerge from the class itself.

12. Marx to Engels, April 12, 1855. *Marx/Engels Werke* (Berlin: Institut für Marxismus-Leninismus, 1963), vol. 28, p. 444.

13. In their jibing at Lassalle, Marx and Engels exhibit in their private letters a nasty anti-Semitism, which has proved the delight of their more liberal bourgeois critics ever since.

14. See Marx's letter to Engels of November 4, 1864 for an account of his tactics in composing the documents. *Marx/Engels Werke*, vol. 31, pp. 9–16.

15. The International's General Council had originally branded Napoleon the aggressor, but now, seeing Prussia's real aims, declared Bismark's war a "war against the French people." In fact, Bismark had originally tricked Bonaparte into the war, but no one, of course, knew this at the time.

16. See Marx's first draft of *The Civil War in France*, available among other places in English translation in Fernbach's *Karl Marx: Political Writings*, vol. 3 (New York: Random House, 1974), pp. 236–68.

17. The term "commune," it should be noted, is the old French designation for any municipality and does not refer to a communist government per se. In designating the new government of Paris a commune, the rebels were not therefore committing themselves to communism.

18. This address was later published as *The Civil War in France*.

19. In his *Critique of the Gotha Program* Marx attacked vigorously the largely Lassallean program the merged groups adopted at the time of the reconciliation.

Chapter Two

1. *The Communist Manifesto*. Though the work is coauthored by Engels, the final draft was completed by Marx and hence bears his mark to a greater degree than that of Engels.

2. This characterization of the relation between increased trade and industrial growth is elsewhere, as we will see—even to some extent in the earlier *German Ideology*—in part reversed, Marx maintaining that manufacture laid the basis for the growth in trade.

3. In describing these stages in the *Manifesto*, Marx uses the term "class" very loosely, identifying the rise of the power of the

cities with the rise of the power of the bourgeoisie as a class. Though it is true, as we will see, that historically this rise of the cities is a prerequisite of bourgeois development, this is somewhat misleading as the classes that controlled the medieval cities were themselves, as the above indicates, largely the victims of bourgeois growth rather than the embryonic form of the capitalist class.

4. These periodic crises appeared in England, the first country to enter the industrial era, as early as the 1820s, less than one hundred years after the industrial revolution took place.

5. This claim of inevitable victory for the proletariat seems, *prima facie* at least, incompatible with the option he has previously posited that leaves open the two possibilities of revolution and mutual ruin of the contending classes. Since the *Manifesto* is essentially a political work, we may want to dismiss the claim as rhetoric and avoid the problem of inconsistency in that way, as those Marxists who, in order to explain Stalinist Russia, hold a "socialism or barbarism" view of current possibilities seem forced to do. However, we should note before jumping to such a conclusion that the mutual ruin alternative is stated in the context of past history alone in the *Manifesto* and that, moreover, there are, on Marx's view, decisive differences between situations such as ancient Roman society where mutual ruin (barbarism) was the result of the class struggle and the situation in capitalist society. The modern proletariat seems to Marx to have achieved an independent development which the ancient proletariat could never accomplish, while the conflict between social relations and productive forces which Marx, as we will see, finds decisive in ushering in positive social transformation, likewise is thought by him to be developing in capitalism, unlike ancient society where it never—at least in any constructive fashion—did. Finally, if we still feel compelled to dismiss the claim as mere political rhetoric, it must be recognized that it reappears elsewhere in Marx at both a later date and in a more theoretical and less political work. See *Capital* (New York: International Publishers, 1967), I, 488.

6. *A Contribution to the Critique of Political Economy* (Moscow: Progress Publishers, 1970), p. 21.

7. From the "Grundrisse" notebooks, the chapter on capital, in the subsection entitled "Formen die der kapitalistischen produktion vorhergehen." Throughout this chapter I have used Hobsbawm's translation, included in his anthology, *Pre-Capitalist Economic Formations* (New York: International Publishers, 1965). See pp. 68–69 for the reference above. An English translation of the "Formen" can also be found in Martin Nicolaus's *Grundrisse*

(Harmondsworth: Penguin Books, 1973) beginning on p. 471 of that work.

8. See "Grundrisse" and *The German Ideology* (New York: International Publishers, 1947), p. 9. This latter work is coauthored by Engels. Note that here as elsewhere Marx does not insist on taking the form of work organization as in any sense prior to social organization.

9. Thus, despite the fears of his more naive critics, community of property, both past and future, in no way entails that we had or shall have, for example, to squeeze into one another's shoes.

10. In an 1881 letter to Vera Sassulitsch (See Hobsbawm, pp. 142–45) Marx refers to this mode as "the last word of the *archaic formation* of societies." The below account, except where otherwise noted, is found in its entirety in the "Grundrisse." At the time of their writing the *German Ideology* neither Marx nor Engels had researched "Asian" property relations.

11. Such cooperation can be seen most clearly in the division of labor between men and women which is nearly universal; social ties easily override, in all but the most sophisticated of societies, the cleavage of interests that such a division forms. I have, incidentally, in the above used the phrase "social division of labor" in a different sense than Marx does in the first chapter of *Capital* where he claims (I, 42) that a social division does exist in the Indian village; he is in this passage using the term as synonymous with "division of labor" per se.

12. This discussion should help to clarify the claims made by Marx in *The German Ideology* (for example, on p. 49) that class formation and the division of labor are the same phenomenon.

13. Letter to Engels, March 14, 1868. *Marx/Engels Werke*, Vol. 32, pp. 42–44. The use of the term "Asiatic" to describe these ancient European forms is perhaps an extension of its original use, which, as I have indicated, seems to encompass only the most socially and technically advanced of communal societies. The "form of village communities built upon the common ownership of land" though it had disappeared in China by Marx's day and was fast undergoing dissolution under the British in India was, Marx claims, the original form in both of these civilizations; see *Capital*, III, 333–34.

14. This, of course, cannot in itself account for the emergence of ancient society as it already presupposes the existence of forces tending toward disintegration of the communal form.

15. *The German Ideology*, p. 11. In its original use in Rome the term "proletarian" referred to those citizens who, being propertyless,

had nothing to offer the state but their *proles* or offspring—who were useful, at most, as soldiers in a professional army.

16. Ibid., pp. 10–11.

17. When Hobsbawm thus complains (p. 40) that in the "Grundrisse" Marx fails to discuss "the actual economic contradictions of a slave economy" treating them as "merely a special aspect of the fundamental contradiction of ancient society," he is looking for contradictions that Marx himself never thought to exist. Slavery does in the ancient mode play merely the role of such an "aspect" of the dynamic. We may for this reason be ill advised in calling the slaves a class at all—at least in the narrowest meaning of the term.

18. *The German Ideology*, p.11.

19. Ibid., p. 20. See also the preface to *A Contribution to the Critique of Political Economy* (Moscow: Progress Publishers, 1970).

20. Marx is at no point very specific concerning these developments, but it seems the ability to get its dole as much as anything must have been the chief issue around which the debilitating class war between plebs and patres revolved at this time.

21. Letter to Sassulitsch, March 8, 1881. See Hobsbawm, p. 144.

22. *The German Ideology*, p. 11.

23. Though Marx nowhere mentions it, the Roman institution of the "client" who worked the patrician's land as tenant farmer rather than slave also apparently influenced the institution of serfdom. As for the German migrations themselves, it is believed today that they resulted largely from pressures of people to the east, notably the Huns, who were themselves being pressured by a strengthened and expanding Chinese Empire. Some free peasants and peasants in only semidependency do, it should also be noted, persist through the entire feudal period, perpetuating the "popular life" we have quoted Marx as referring to above.

24. For an interesting account of the battles over this public land in England in the early years of the capitalist epoch see Christopher Hill's *The World Turned Upside Down* (New York: Viking, 1972).

25. See *The German Ideology*, pp. 12–13, 44–47.

26. This account, though taken from *The German Ideology*, an earlier work than the *Communist Manifesto*, besides fitting the facts of medieval history better, also, as we shall see, squares better with Marx's later accounts of medieval society and its transition to the bourgeois mode.

27. *Capital*, III, 801.

28. Ibid., p. 332. There are, however, Marx notes, considerable differences even within the ancient world with regard to craft

development's accompaniment of increased trade, Greece, for example, showing a stronger development than late republican Rome.

29. Marx in fact says in his correspondence that any account of the motion of history would be suspiciously "mystical" if in it accident never entered into the process.

30. Though, as we shall also see, out of this opposition ultimately will emerge two classes in opposition, the aristocrats and the bourgeoisie; here too, however, the antagonism is more complex than a simple class struggle; for the workers are, as were the slaves and serfs before them, allied with their masters in this struggle against the feudal lords. At times this alliance is an explicit political one but even where this is lacking, it is always present in their role as the labor which underlies bourgeois power.

31. *The German Ideology*, pp. 20–21. As the following discussion indicates, Marx and Engels's claim here that "division of labour and private property are ... identical expressions" is not, with the full development of Marx's work, held by him to be true. In 1846, when the *Ideology* manuscript was completed, he had not begun research on the Asiatic mode, however, and so saw the relation between the two as a far simpler one than that which he later held it to be. It should also be noted that Marx and Engels here, as elsewhere, hold the first "true" division of labor to be that between mental and material labor.

32. *Capital*, I, 714.

33. "Grundrisse," Hobsbawm's translation of the "Formen" section, p. 69.

34. *Capital*, III, 332.

35. *The German Ideology*, p. 50, and "Grundrisse" (Hobsbawm, p. 112). Note how clearly here the general formula of a clash between social relations (relations of production) and productive forces is invoked to explain social revolution. For this disparity is the *sine qua non* in Marx's account of the bourgeois revolution. Much of the accumulated commercial wealth [with the exception, of course, of stolen wealth such as the Mesoamerican and Peruvian gold], he points out further in the "Grundrisse," really owes its existence to the developing medieval crafts, as these are exactly what tend to develop trade. He is arguing here in a somewhat partisan fashion against those bourgeois apologists who act as if the initial capital that ushered in the industrial revolution was miraculously produced by the early capitalists themselves, but the point is nonetheless well taken. A similar argument to that in the "Grundrisse" is found in *Capital*, Vol. III, chap. 20; see note 42 below.

36. The following account is found complete only in *The German*

Ideology, pp. 47–58. In all later sources it can be reconstructed only with difficulty from hints and remarks in which it is only implicitly contained.

37. *Capital,* I, 336.

38. Ibid., p. 322.

39. Ibid., see pp. 336–50 for all quotes, unless otherwise noted, in the following discussion.

40. Ibid., p. 326.

41. An exception to the former can, of course, occur when the new organization of work itself calls into being the need for new skills.

42. *Capital,* III, 332–33. The reasons for Marx's somewhat extreme insistence on priority of manufacture over commerce here have already been to some extent discussed in the text. Both the fact that Marx sees the development of medieval craft as the difference between ancient and feudal potentialities and the, previously mentioned, *political* need to discredit those who argued that labor does not create capitalism, since it does not produce the initial capital invested in industry, seem to influence Marx's remarks here. Perhaps also the fact that such a view conforms to the forces versus relations formula is at work as well. At any rate, however the emphasis is placed, the relation between commerce and industry is a reciprocal one—each bolstering the other as they simultaneously develop; this is at all times clear in everything that Marx says. In point of fact, he even readily admits (*Capital,* I, 754) that commercial supremacy in the period of manufacture determines industrial supremacy for a nation, the converse only obtaining later, in contradistinction to, though I believe not in contradiction of, some of the remarks quoted above. Portugal, with no manufacture, may not be able to use its commercial wealth, but commercial wealth is the decisive factor once manufactures are present. The *Manifesto* account, as we have seen, is even more one-sided in its emphasis on commerce, though even in it Marx sees modern industry as having "established the world market."

43. The entire account, except where noted, is taken from "The So-Called Primitive Accumulation," *Capital,* vol. I, pt. 8. Marx's irony, wasted often on petty matters, here finds a subject worthy of its power; his writing is consequently at its best, vivid, and without a trace of either rhetorical cant or professorial pedantry.

44. Marx himself nowhere clearly presents this or any other account of the disappearance of serfdom, but the account I have given is of a relatively uncontroversial textbook variety. See, for

KARL MARX

example, that of Crane Brinton in his *History of Civilization*
(Englewood Cliffs: Prentice Hall, 1955), I, 269.

45. On the Continent, where bourgeois political power was secured
much later, the rule of force continued to be the chief means of
expropriation far longer than in Britian. The alliance of gentry and
capitalists in England, in lieu of political struggle, seems to be the
chief factor in its accelerated development; a commercially minded
"modern" gentry had early replaced the old nobility which "had
been devoured by the great [English] feudal wars."

46. It is sadly ironical that during the period of primitive accumulation in the Soviet Union, Stalin used a state power in the
name of Marxian socialism itself to accomplish much the same
task; it also reiterates Marx and Engels's warning that to look at
what men say about themselves rather than what they do will not
lead to a true understanding of society; it is incredible that such a
relatively small number of contemporary "Marxists" are able to take
this advice.

47. *Capital*, I, 270–302, gives a full account of legislation concerning the working day in England and elsewhere during the
entire tenure of capitalism.

48. *Capital*, I, 745–49.

49. Hobsbawm, pp. 116–17; the best presentation of the entire
discussion is found here.

50. At least so Marx believed in the 1858 "Grundrisse" notebooks. With the growing world market, we might wonder if this is
an absolute prerequisite in view of the previously established independent development of the towns. The first manufactures were,
after all, for this export market, and it seems not unlikely that—
even in the absence of rural manufacture—they would have continued to grow. At any rate, the whole process was most certainly
accelerated by its involvement in the countryside; growth rate and
the continued opening of the world market would have both lagged
considerably in its absence.

51. *Capital*, I, 751, 759–60. In the "Grundrisse," Marx, in contradistinction to his remarks here, speaks of American plantation
slavery as an anomaly within a market based on free labor; but I
believe he is talking there of the slavery of the nineteenth century,
not that of the eighteenth, which he felt was still part and parcel
of capitalist development and not in the least an abberation in the
system.

52. The whole of the below discussion is found in *Capital*, vol. I,
chap. 15. A shorter but, in part at least, substantially similar account
can be found already in the *Communist Manifesto*. Much of Marx's

critique of the conditions of labor under capitalism in fact is drawn from Wilhelm Schulz, the radical economist, whom he quotes extensively in the *1844 Manuscripts*. Note here that Marx, perhaps due to his own class limitations, tends to downgrade the role of the women in the struggle. A predominantly male leadership, which in actuality may not in all instances have been present in these early years, is usually assumed as both a fact and a necessity.

53. Many of the weavers, Marx notes, in fact starved to death; others were forced to emigrate. The introduction of machinery provided in practice a great spur to colonization. It also forced many foreign nations and colonies into the position of being producers of raw materials alone; once established by the accidents of development, moreover, this situation was often forcibly maintained; India, for example, was prevented by Britain from developing a clothing industry and forced by law to ship raw cloth to the mother country for processing through much of its colonial history.

54. See Chapter 6 for an account of the argument for this tendency.

55. The modern industrial assembly line which tends to reestablish manufacture organization in an industrial setting was in Marx's time not yet in existence.

56. Marx thus apparently recognizes these specialists as a part of labor at the same time that he recognizes a profound split here. Surely, as we will see, there seems—many Marxists to the contrary— no way to maintain that they are not wage workers in the service of capital and hence part of the class; Marx himself, far more liberal than his followers, is wont on occasion to include even salaried management in the worker category.

57. *The Communist Manifesto,* sect. 1.

Chapter Three

1. This quote from *The Civil War in France* is, as we shall see, somewhat specific to the particular situation, but it still serves adequately to illustrate the point made here.

2. *The Communist Manifesto,* sect. 3. See also the discussion in the following chapter of B. F. Skinner's contemporary utopian approach.

3. Buckminster Fuller provides perhaps an even better example than Skinner of reactionary utopianism in a contemporary setting; his combining of an intense interest in the future of mankind with intense paranoia with regard to any attempts to mold that future— for example, his belief that the student movement of the 1960s

was planned in Moscow and/or Peking—provides a striking example for Marx's evaluation of latter day utopian tendencies.

4. The term "communism" is usually used by Marx to refer to both the future classless society and the transitional workers' state. On occasion in his mature works, however, he uses it to refer exclusively to the former while in the early *1844 Manuscripts* where it is called "the negation of private property" it seems, on the contrary, *at times*, to refer only to transitional forms. "Socialism" is also, it should be noted, used primarily as a synonym for "communism" by Marx, though some Marxian socialist writers identify it with the workers' state, reserving the term "communism" for the classless future.

5. *The Economic and Philosophical Manuscripts of 1844.* I have used here, and throughout the book, T. B. Bottomore's translation as found in his *Karl Marx: Early Writings* (New York: McGraw-Hill, 1963), pp. 155–67.

6. *The German Ideology*, pp. 74, 20–22. Though the *1844 Manuscripts* also concern themselves with the division of labor they do so mainly in the context of a critique of nineteenth-century political economy; the theme is more clearly developed in the context of Marx's historical views here.

7. *The German Ideology*, p. 44.

8. Ibid., p. 22. The fact that the passage is not supposed to be a literal description of communist society should be clear; the reference to Young Hegelian "critical critics" in itself points to its satiric nature. Marx and Engels have too clear an understanding of— as well as contempt for—agrarian Romantic nostalgia to be waxing enthusiastic along such lines here.

9. Note that here something of a view of "human nature" seems to be present in Marx's work; it is, as we shall see below, still present as late as the writing of *Capital*. These facts will prove of importance when we come to the discussion of the relation between Marx's late and early work in Chapter 5.

10. *Capital*, I, 487. It is thus stressed here, not that communism requires the abolition of the division of labor, but that the abolition of the division of labor—being necessary under conditions of modern industry—requires communism. This, of course, in no way entails that the former is not also true. Hence, the account in *Capital* given above may, if we wish to see it, be viewed as a supplement to the original *German Ideology* account. A reference in the still later (1875) *Critique of the Gotha Program* to the division of labor as "enslaving" may be read in fact as reiterating the early claim, thus strengthening such a position on the matter.

11. *Capital*, I, 488. Lest we see this reference to the compulsion of modern industry as a form of technological determinism, we should bear in mind that industry's "compulsion" here is but a medium for the desire of the laboring masses working *under the limitations of that industry* to maintain and perhaps to improve upon their conditions of life in the face of capitalism's supposed impotence to much longer do so.

12. *Capital*, III, 820; italics mine. Note once again the allusion to "human nature" at this late date.

13. The actual labor expended in all activity will decrease as the forces of production—which are, as will become even more evident in Chapter 6, fettered by the capitalist system—come to be freely developed; even aside from this, however, the labor expended in the "realm of necessity" is, of course, in any system only a part of total labor, so that free time must necessarily increase when only necessary labor is subjected to any compulsion. The speculation below, I should add, though based on these Marxist premises, is entirely my own and not to be found anywhere in Marx's work itself.

14. *The German Ideology*, pp. 74–75.

15. Ibid., pp. 23–24. Marx also adds here that the claim of representation of the general interest is usually strengthened by the existence of real cultural ties among the population. His analysis of the state in terms of class rule does not blind him to this very important fact.

16. A surprising number of Marxists do, however, fail to see just this, insofar as they mistake the assertion that the class struggle is played out politically in part within bourgeois politics for the social democrats' assertion that it has its resolution there. Holding themselves aloof from even the contemplation of actual political development, they may remain pure, but only by way of a thorough distortion of the reality which surrounds them. And then they rail at those poor brainwashed folk who cannot see the social world through their dogmatic lenses!

17. *The Communist Manifesto*, sect. 2.

18. See Marx's *Critique of the Gotha Program*, sect. 1. The slogan, though quoted by Marx, is not original with him but originates with the followers of Saint Simon.

19. Ibid., sect. 1.

20. *The German Ideology*, p. 76. In the earlier *Introduction to the Critique of Hegel's Philosophy of Right* the language is more rhetorical, the proletariat being described as having experienced "a total loss of humanity" and thereby only being able to "redeem itself by a total redemption of humanity"; but the substance is, I believe, the

same. Note that "property" in the above as elsewhere, refers to productive property alone.

21. *The German Ideology*, p. 75.

22. *The Communist Manifesto*, sect. 2.

23. Shlomo Avinieri, *The Social and Political Thought of Karl Marx*, (London: Cambridge Univ. Press, 1968), p. 206.

24. *Capital*, I, 406–7. It is interesting to note that these problems, so vivid in contemporary debate, were evident to some at least even a hundred years ago.

25. Bottomore, pp. 153–55.

26. *The Communist Manifesto*, sect. 2.

27. Marx to F. Domela-Nieuwenhuis, February 22, 1881. *Marx/Engels Werke*, vol. 35, p. 160. A German idiom which Marx uses in the letter, "ins Bockshorn zu jagen" (literally, to hunt Hartshorn or *fenugreek*, a wild herb) signifies generally the act of frightening. Saul Padover's translation of "without frightening," which we find in his multivolumed anthology of Marx's work, thus has Marx holding a view opposite to that which he here holds.

28. *The Civil War in France*, chap. 3. Note here that Marx is not, like many anarchist theorists, applauding decentralization for its own sake, but simply as a means to a desired end.

29. By 1875, after German unification had been accomplished, he appears to have adopted this view of state power in Germany as well. For in the *Critique of the Gotha Program* he writes: "Free state—what is this? . . . Freedom consists in converting the state from an organ superimposed on society into one completely subordinate to it, and today, too, the forms of state are more or less free to the extent that they restrict the 'freedom of the state.'"

30. From the first draft for *The Civil War in France*, reprinted in Fernbach, p. 253.

31. *The Civil War in France*, chap. 3. Marx speculates also that, had it had time to implement its full plan for France, it might have rallied the peasants round it as well.

32. See also Avinieri's account which, though I believe it exaggerates Marx's concessions to popular left-wing sentiment concerning the Commune in framing the final draft of *The Civil War in France*, in essentials parallels my own.

33. It is interesting to note, however, that in an 1872 address to the International he says that a simultaneous rising in other European cities could have secured the Commune's rule.

34. There are other references to be found in *The German Ideology* but, as stated here, they seem too general to be fruitfully included in

our survey and fail to add anything to what we have already seen Marx's views to be.

35. *Critique of the Gotha Program,* sect. 3.

36. This is not to say, however, that it inhibits the growth of the social product itself in any *simple* fashion—that is, it is not a denial of the fact that the product under capitalism will grow.

37. *Capital,* III, 83. The system of labor certificates explained below can perhaps serve to further clarify Marx's remarks here.

38. If it is in fact not to be, the radical disruption of wage differentials would, I would think, in the initial phases of socialism cause undue disruption within the working class itself; workers, who had won through previous struggle higher than average gains, would, it seems reasonable to suppose, balk at a sudden reduction to the social average. Perhaps, however, Marx is aware of this and simply speaking of the condition of the average laborer. In a subsequent paragraph he equates the labor credits involved with "value" which, we will see, is very definitely weighted according to skill. At any rate, he is certainly in the vast bulk of his writings no proto-Maoist appealing on moral grounds for members of the class to surrender positions of relative privilege, but an opponent of such moralism, who accepts only the values which emerge from the class itself as it develops.

39. In Engels's writings we find, in addition to the 1850 document which he also signed, six further references to it—making a grand total of fourteen in the work of the two men.

40. Hal Draper, "Marx and the Dictatorship of the Proletariat," *New Politics* 1, no. 4 (Summer, 1962), 95–104.

41. See *Critique of the Gotha Program,* sect. 4.

42. Engels in fact clearly states, again in 1891, that the dictatorship of the proletariat itself will and must have the "democratic republic" for its form.

43. One piece of evidence which may weigh against this interpretation should, however, in fairness be acknowledged. In the early *1844 Manuscripts* Marx seems to leave open both possibilities for the first phase of communism, describing it as either "democratic or despotic," though even here the despotism in question may simply be inter- and not intraclass.

44. *Critique of the Gotha Program,* sect. 4.

45. The 1852 *Daily Tribune* reference to the Chartists which Avinieri (p. 214) cites does not discount force, since it is a purely hypothetical statement, a "what if the English working class gained suffrage." Likewise, in the 1867 statement contained in a speech on the Polish insurrection (p. 215) he only repeats in essence the view I cite below from *Capital.* It seems not in fact to be true that Marx,

as Avinieri claims, "never visualized a violent revolution in England."
He in fact *always* held it to be *possible* there.

46. *Capital*, I, 751.

47. Ibid., p. 764.

48. Ibid., p. 9. Marx is here thinking specifically of England. He seems, however, never to have held it as certain that the scenario would occur in precisely this way; the opinion here is, that is to say, strictly speculation in the fashion of 1867.

49. Speech to the International, The Hague, September 15, 1872. Reprinted in Fernbach, p. 324.

50. Letter to Henry Hyndman, Dec. 8, 1880. *Marx/Engels Werke*, vol. 34, p. 482.

51. Circular letter to their associates in the Party, September 17, 1879. Ibid., p. 402.

52. Letter to Bolte, November 23, 1871. *Marx/Engels Werke*, vol. 33, pp. 332–33.

53. M. Bookchin, "Listen, Marxist!" originally privately printed; reprinted in his *Post-Scarcity Anarchism* (Berkeley: Ramparts, 1971), p. 183. Bookchin's further insistence here on limiting the proletariat to include industrial workers only is a practice in which I do not follow him in the discussion below nor anywhere else in this book.

54. Ibid., p. 180. See also Herbert Marcuse, *One Dimensional Man* (Boston: Beacon Press, 1964), chap. 1.

Chapter Four

1. For Engels on materialism see especially *Dialectics of Nature* and *Anti-Duhring* and the 1892 introduction to *Socialism: Utopian & Scientific*.

2. I am thinking here of Avinieri, especially, who never ceases to delight in contrasting the humanistic dialectician Marx with the supposedly "bloody-minded" mechanist, Engels.

3. *A Contribution to the Critique of Political Economy*, p. 20. The preface also alludes to a view which has sometimes been read as a species of technological determinism (for example, by Karl Popper). As the full exposition of Marx's views will easily show this to be a misinterpretation, however, we can safely ignore this further problem here. For a detailed criticism of the technological determinist interpretation, the reader is referred to Bernard Gendron's "Marx and the Technological Theory of History," *Philosophical Forum* vol. 6, no. 4, (Summer, 1976), pp. 397–422.

4. The *Theses on Feuerbach* were first published by Engels in 1888 but written, as we have seen, in 1845. The above claim is also repeated seven years later in the *18th Brumaire of Louis Bonaparte*

(New York: International Publishers, 1963), p. 15. Engels too makes much the same observation nearly fifty years later in a letter to Joseph Bloch.

5. Skinner in fact, with an arrogance which may be matched only by his naiveté, claims that he has described scientifically the process which Marx described in a "crude way" as the class struggle. See *Beyond Freedom and Dignity* (New York: Bantam/Vintage, 1972), pp. 133–34.

6. See the May 9, 1868 letter to Dietzgen (*Marx/Engels Werke*, 32, p. 547) in which Marx tells of his plan to eventually write an essay on dialectics which will strip the subject of its Hegelian "mystical form" and his similar disclosure to Engels in a letter of January 16, 1858 (*Werke*, 29, p. 260) that he wants to publish a few papers which will turn Hegel's "mystery" back into "common sense."

7. A good account of the relationship of formal and dialectical logic can be found in Henri Lefebvre's *Dialectical Materialism* (London: Jonathan Cape, 1968), pp. 41–43.

8. Hegel in the *Phenomenology of Mind* in fact provides a critique of teleological explanation as mistaking internal purposiveness for external pull.

9. Marx, *Critique of Hegel's Doctrine of the State* in R. Livingstone and G. Benton's *Karl Marx: Early Writings* (Baltimore: Penguin, 1975), p. 65. The italics here are mine.

10. Note that for certain purposes where dialectics are not essential to understanding we can regard both concepts and things in isolation; formal logic and mechanistic science, the products of what Hegel has called "understanding," are not rejected but subsumed in the dialectical view.

11. Hegel, *Science of Logic,* trans. W.H. Johnston and L.G. Struthers (New York: Macmillan, 1929), part I.

12. Bottomore, p. 199. Actually, much of the work that Marx made use of in Hegel was developed more fully by Hegel in writings which preceded the *Phenomenology*, but Marx was unfamiliar with the writings of this period. See Marcuse's *Reason and Revolution* (Boston: Beacon Press, 1960) for a full discussion of this point.

13. *The Phenomenology of Mind,* trans. James Baillie (New York: Harper & Row, 1967), p. 149.

14. Ibid., p. 210. Note the influence of Kant's transcendental idealism here.

15. Pursuing further the analog between Hegel's account of consciousness and the linguistic philosophy of the Wittgensteinians, it is interesting to note that this recognition that consciousness (or language in use) is a social phenomenon, which is almost a mere

starting point for Hegel, is the end all and be all for ordinary language philosophy. The relationship between language (consciousness) and the society which produces and uses it is not seen as a fit subject for philosophical investigation by linguistic philosophers and hence the political uses of language are by them ignored. Language with political antecedents not being so recognized inevitably presents the present political situation as permanent; hence the small amount of political philosophy which has come out of the ordinary language movement has been basically conservative. Moreover, lacking any concept of language as dynamic, in disanalogy with Hegel's dynamic Mind, ordinary language philosophy has heretofore failed to study linguistic change, even as Hegel can, that is, retrospectively, instead treating the categories of contemporary usage in certain strata of society as eternal and inviolable categories of the world in which all distinctions can be made and all wisdom lies submerged (see, for example, J.L. Austin's work). This, of course, even further intensifies the conservatism which results from a failure to grasp the political aspects of language.

16. Hegel, *The Phenomenology of Mind,* pp. 229–40.

17. Paul Sweezy, *Monthly Review* (April, 1975), vol. 26, p. 13.

18. The following discussion is found in the *Phenomenology,* Chapter V, sect. B, to Chapter VIII.

19. *Outline of the Philosophy of Right.* Hegel also dealt at less length with the material presented here four years earlier in his *Encyclopedia of the Philosophical Sciences.*

20. Hegel, introduction to *The Philosophy of Right.*

21. Ibid., preface. This limitation becomes even more apparent in a philosophy such as contemporary linguistic analysis, which fails to comprehend the dynamic aspects of thought or language.

22. Bottomore, pp. 211–12. Marx's discussion here makes reference repeatedly to the notion of alienation. As this topic will be considered in Chapter 5, I will at this point ignore this aspect of his critique of Hegel, I trust without damage or distortion of his meaning. As to my extensive use of this and other relatively early works in this section on method, I believe it to be justified in presenting Marx's mature views as well, in that he himself as late as 1873 acknowledges his early critique of Hegel in an Afterward to the second German edition of *Capital.*

23. Bottomore, p. 202.

24. Ibid., p. 201.

25. Ibid., p. 211.

26. Hegel, *The Phenomenology of Mind,* p. 247.

27. I have in fact found only one author, Joel Carmichael in his

Karl Marx (New York: Scribners, 1973) who blatantly misunderstands the Marxian dialectic, accusing Marx of a formal contradiction at a point in *Capital* where a dialectical interaction is being explained.

28. *Capital*, I, 19–20. The quotes are taken from an afterword to the second German edition of the book.

29. The below quote is found in Bottomore, p. 214; see also the discussion in Marx's 1843 *Critique of Hegel's Doctrine of the State*. I do not here mean to imply that the Feuerbachian transformation is identical with that of Marx. As we shall see, Marx is at pains to distinguish himself from Feuerbach as well as the materialists who preceded him.

30. Bottomore, p. 216.

31. Ibid., pp. 206–7.

32. *Theses on Feuerbach*, thesis one.

33. *The German Ideology*, p. 7.

34. *The Communist Manifesto*, sect. 1.

35. See Chapter 6, especially sections 4 and 5.

36. These features of dialectical analysis were first made clear to me in an early draft of Milton Fisk's "Rate of Profit and Class Struggle," *Radical Philosophers' Newsjournal*, no. 5 (August 1975), pp. 1–37. It becomes important to remember the last, Professor Fisk demonstrates, when one is tempted to read Marx in *Capital* as an economist who is making straightforward claims about trends in the economy; such claims fail to be straightforward (mechanistic) in Marx in that they invariably reflect only the movement of one pole of a dialectical interaction. Again, for a more concrete account, the reader should turn to Chapter 6.

37. This of course in no way entails that it is not still the best theory available to deal with the subject it examines. Also, it should be noted that not all useful theories based on a mechanistic methodology involve themselves in precise prediction. Biological evolution does not, for example, allow one to trace either predictively or retrodictively the course of the development of species in any precise fashion; even within mechanistic science, to use classical physics as one's paradigm introduces a rigidity which is unwarranted—all the more so as the modern physical paradigm (quantum mechanics) is only probabilistic, at least in its microscopic results.

38. Marcuse, *Reason and Revolution*, p. 340. Bottomore in the introduction to his translation of Marx's early writings presents a succinct, clear, and intelligent reply to this interpretation of Marx which supplements my own. He also discusses the variants of it due to Lukács and Gramsci at more length in the introduction to his an-

thology, *Karl Marx* (Englewood Cliffs: Prentice Hall, 1973), pp. 36–39.

39. A. Comte, *Cours de Philosophie Positive*, vol. 4, 4th edition (Paris, 1877), p. 267.

40. In its twentieth-century form it reaches a totalitarian apotheosis of conservatism in the neopositivism and behaviorism which Marcuse has very ably exposed in his *One Dimensional Man* (Boston: The Beacon Press, 1964). As struggle intensifies, as we shall see, the liberal spirit of the young bourgeoisie grows increasingly crabbed and gives way to a need for greater and greater control. Classical materialism as its ideology has moved a long way from its auspicious beginnings in which it had, as Marx says in *The Holy Family*, a necessary connection with communism.

41. Marcuse, *Reason and Revolution*, pp. 312–20. In speaking of "demystification" here, I refer to the Hegelian baggage replete with "transcendent" viewpoint which Marcuse would have Marx carry with him throughout his working life.

42. Given this, certain supplementary theories are in fact of great potential utility to the Marxist theoretician. Wilhelm Reich's early social psychology, for example, though—in view of its acceptance of the myth of working class complicity in German Fascism—I would by no means want to give it my unqualified approval, presents an interesting case in point. Knowledge from any of the social and even the biological sciences can, if skillfully used, always enhance practice; to fail to utilize it where possible would involve one in a dogmatic application of Marxist theory of a sort which our analysis has clearly indicated unwarranted.

43. It should be added here that an application of dialectics in empirical social theory is not by any means limited to either studies of the full social realm or those which center around a Marxian schema. Paul Feyerabend has, for example, sketched a non-Marxian dialectical account of the growth of science in his very interesting essay, "Consolations for the Specialist," published in Alan Musgrave and Imre Lakatos's *Criticism and the Growth of Knowledge*, (London: Cambridge University Press, 1970) pp. 197–230; a comparison of this essay with Marx's work should widen one's understanding and appreciation of the technique considerably.

44. It is, of course, far beyond the scope of this book to consider the functionalist alternative. If we were to entertain functional accounts in the biological sciences, however, it is interesting to note that there are several biological phenomena which lend themselves easily to dialectical accounts. Like death, the transformation of a lake into a swamp as the result of the struggle between its—nonetheless

interdependent—plant and animal life, provides perhaps the most perfect case in point.

45. A more complete discussion of science and ideology in Marx can be found in Chapter 6.

46. *The German Ideology,* p. 71.

47. *Capital,* I, 372. Lest one think that this passage also further implies a technological determinism, I should note that in context it is clear that technology here is being recommended as a concrete indicator of a society's material life, not as its ultimate cause. To read the passage in any other way would be to impose a mechanistic structure on Marx.

48. Bottomore, p. 162.

49. Ibid., p. 156. It is clear from these passages that the materialistic approach, even in its most extreme formulations, is not a post-1844 innovation as defenders of the "mature" Marx, such as Althusser in his *For Marx* (New York: Random House, 1970), maintain.

50. See Engels's letter to Joseph Bloch, September 21–22, 1890, *Marx/Engels Werke,* vol. 37, pp. 462–65; also the letter to Conrad Schmidt, October 27, 1890 (ibid., pp. 488-95), and that to W. Borgius, January 25, 1894, *Werke,* vol. 39, pp. 205–207. See also his *Ludwig Feuerbach and the End of Classical German Philosophy* where —though I have not, as I have said, made use herein of his analysis— many of the points made in this chapter seem to be confirmed.

Chapter Five

1. See Althusser, *For Marx* and Bell, "The Rediscovery of Alienation," *Journal of Philosophy* 61, (November 19, 1959) pp. 934–50. I do not in calling Althusser an apologist intend to imply that he is not at times a very perceptive scholar; when he is not simply rationalizing the latest party line, his brilliance, as well as his knowledge of Marxism, is always evident. Bell's scholarly merits with regard to this subject are, as we shall see, somewhat more suspect.

2. Bottomore, p. 121. The notion of a continuing progressive emiseration of labor, which is here expressed, is discussed in detail in the next chapter. The second claim, that the worker becomes a cheaper commodity as he creates more, is, it should be noted, independent of the former in that prices generally drop with increased productivity along with the drop in the price of labor; of course, in this process, skilled and semiskilled labor are replaced progressively by simple, unskilled labor so that in this sense yesterday's skilled workman is constantly being undermined and impoverished by the new arrangements of the day; in context, it may perhaps be to this that Marx here refers; the question of his actual views on the sub-

ject of changes in living standards is, as we shall see, wrapped in obscurity. Finally, the observation that the worker produces himself as commodity refers to the fact that his production within the commodity form necessitates his absorption as a commodity for sale on the market—in this case the labor market—along with other items in this form.

3. Ibid., p. 129. The concept of alienation, of course, just as that of objectification, has its origins in Hegelian philosophy. It is taken from there by Marx via the use which Feuerbach put it to in his "inverted" version of Hegel where he argues for atheism on the ground that God is man's own being in alienation, a superstitious projection of his own potential. In fact, throughout the *Manuscripts,* Marx, still greatly influenced by Feuerbach, is at pains to show that his own view of alienation of labor encompasses and supercedes the Feuerbachian theological alienation, that "the quest for an *alien* being . . . above man and nature" will cease with the abolition of labor's alienation in communism and only with it.

4. The below is a paraphrase of material in Bottomore, pp. 125–26.

5. Ibid., p. 126–29.

6. Ibid., p. 181.

7. The account which Bell, and Harrington following him ("Marx versus Marx," *New Politics* [Fall, 1961] pp. 112–123), give of Marx's views on alienation—that through it men lose (1) "control over the *conditions* of work" and (2) "the *product* of their labor"—can thus be seen to be entirely inadequate. What it misses in fact seems to be exactly those aspects of Marxian alienation which have interested humanists most—self-estrangement, species estrangement, and estrangement among men. Bell's further assessment of what remains of his simplified version of alienation in the later Marx is equally crude; but I shall return to that later.

8. Bottomore, pp. 177–78. We might perhaps see this fifth aspect as subsumed under the third; it seems at least to be able to be derived from it.

9. Note that alienation of labor exists for Marx in even what he was later to regard as preclass, communalistic forms (India, Mexico), though he may include these only because he has not yet the view of them which his subsequent studies will provide.

10. This early formulation of method, the understanding of institutions and legal arrangements in terms of social relations, characterizes also the approach of all Marx's subsequent work.

11. Bottomore, p. 132. This may, it is interesting to note, provide the key to the above-mentioned notion of alienation in the preclass

Asiatic form. For just as here society is seen as abstract capitalist and relations of alienation still obtain, there it is seen in the form of abstract deities; the monuments to these deities are an alienated expression of social unity.

12. Ibid., pp. 139–40; se also p. 152.

13. Ibid., p. 180.

14. *The Communist Manifesto*, sect. 1.

15. Bottomore, 156–62.

16. The expression of his "materialist" viewpoint, always difficult for Marx, seems extremely clumsily put here in this earliest attempt at an economic critique.

17. Bottomore, pp. 193–94.

18. Ibid., p. 189. Though this process of increasing the productivity of labor may, under capitalism, be seen as part and parcel of the intensification of alienation, and hence to be subsumed under it, it has a certain independence of it, at least in the sense that capitalism, though a sufficient condition for such increase, is not a necessary one; the productive forces can grow also under nonalienated conditions once the epitome of alienated development has laid the ground for it.

19. Harrington, p. 120, in answering Bell's claim that these are mere "literary and illustrative references," notes that approximately one quarter of the first volume of *Capital* involves a discussion of this characteristic of work under capitalism.

20. *Critique of the Gotha Program*, sect. 1. "Work" here thus, it should be reiterated, refers to an activity which is voluntarily undertaken and has a sense other than that which is its primary one today.

21. We can see easily from the above that Bell's version of the carry-over from the *Manuscripts* is as inadequate as his characterization of alienation has been; surely, far more remains in Marx's later work than a complaint of loss of job control and the fact of exploitation.

22. If one's only need is to show that Marx is a humanist, then one could easily let his case rest here; he also could, of course, make a nearly comparable case without reference to the early writings—for the only thing they seem to add to the later accounts of communism is the *explicit* acknowledgment that communism is a humanism.

23. In the *Manuscripts*' supplementary (or, these being unfinished manuscripts, possibly alternative) account of capitalism's development of wealth as a prerequisite for supercession, it should be noted, that alienation is again involved—as a force, as it were, waiting in abeyance, to make its presence felt in history, when the solution of the problem of scarcity is at last in sight.

24. I find a possible exception to this in the "Grundrisse" (Hobs-

bawm, p. 84) where true wealth, once the "narrow bourgeois form has been peeled away," is described, along with other things—including free activity—as consisting in "human control over the forces of nature." If here we read true "wealth" as meaning full human development and "control over nature" as humanization of the world we seem to have something very close to essence as species-being. It should be added, however, that, even granting this, such references never appear after this time in Marx; and that, moreover, even here such a concept of essence, if present at all, does not function as a part of a social dynamic; rather, it is merely brought in as an aside to explain modern nostalgia for the ancient world's view of *man*, instead of wealth per se, as the end of social endeavors. (See the discussion below on essence as a dynamic force.)

25. On the *Manuscripts'* view this no doubt is in some sense equivalent to the notion of essence as species-being since, as we saw, the division of labor, the negation of free, varied activity, is said there to be the "expression" of (necessary and sufficient condition for?) alienated species-activity. There is, however, no indication in Marx that this connection is still maintained by him in his subsequent work.

26. Note with reference to this the allusion to "human nature" in the extended passage from the third volume of *Capital* (p. 820) which I previously quoted. Though it perhaps also refers to job variety, it undoubtedly primarily refers to conditions of labor which are fit for a human being.

27. Bottomore, p. 155. "Self-alienation" is in context here, I should add, clearly equivalent to "species-alienation"; the reference is not merely limited to estrangement from productive activity per se.

28. L. Althusser, "Marxism and Humanism," in *For Marx*, p. 227.

29. Marx, "Theses on Feuerbach," thesis six.

30. I would nonetheless balk at Althusser's characterization of them as, one and all, "radically new." Implicit in this characterization is the notion that Marx had not developed his views on materialism prior to 1845, an idea which we have already seen to be incorrect, and that the 1844 work is consequently ideological in nature, a conclusion which I likewise, on independent grounds, dispel below.

31. See *The German Ideology*, p. 22.

Chapter Six

1. As we shall see, however, in a very real sense, not just Volume IV, but the work as a whole is precisely this.

2. *Capital*, I, 35.

3. Marx himself, at the beginning of *Capital*, only sets out ex-

plicitly the need to deal with the latter fact—the whole book, as we shall see, can indeed be read as an analysis of the concept of a commodity. I believe, however, for our purposes here, things will be simpler—if less elegant—if the reader keeps both of the above facts in mind from the start.

4. *Capital*, I, 38.

5. Ibid., p. 37. Note that exchange value for Marx is thus divorced almost entirely from what he considers the real substance of wealth.

6. The somewhat metaphysical quality of the demonstration arises from its superficiality; this superficiality lies in the demonstration's abstraction of an economic fact from its social context, as our subsequent exposition will show.

7. *Capital*, I, 39.

8. Ibid., p. 44.

9. For a full discussion of this point, see the appendix to Marx's earlier version of the first part of *Capital*, the 1859 *A Contribution to the Critique of Political Economy*, pp. 209–10.

10. *The Poverty of Philosophy* (New York: International Publishers, 1963), pp. 45–46. Marx here quotes Ricardo who also was well aware of this trivial fact.

11. *Capital*, III, 775.

12. Ibid, p. 178.

13. Ibid., p. 861. It is undoubtedly impossible to determine *a priori* when monopoly ceases to be "limited" and the law of value hence, ceases to govern the system as a whole. Whether it has done so already in contemporary capitalism is a source of much debate among theorists on the left today, as is also the question of what such a change in capitalism would entail.

14. See *Capital*, I, 537.

15. This had been in classical political economy a stumbling block for the labor theory. To see that the employer's labor cannot account for profit we need only note that the feasibility of stock companies, in which control of capital and managerial "productive" effort are fully separate, that is, in which the owners need have no connection with actual production at all, renders impossible this alternative. Marx in fact saw the emergence of these companies in his day as a clarification of class relations. See *Capital*, III, 437.

16. *Capital*, I, 170-73.

17. I speak here of a male worker with dependents, but, of course, throughout much of the capitalist era the entire family beyond a certain age was generally employed; child labor, once more highly prized than adult labor, is probably now permanently a thing of the

past—thanks to the struggles of labor—but we should not let ideology blind us to the fact that women have moved in and out of the work force—usually as a part of capital's efforts to undermine the wage—throughout capitalism's history up to the present time.

18. *Capital,* I, 77.

19. Ibid., pp. 72–83.

20. *Capital,* III, 814–15.

21. "All science would be superfluous," writes Marx, "if the outward appearance and the essence of things directly coincided" (ibid., p. 817).

22. See the chapter on method for a further elaboration of this point.

23. *Capital,* I, 73–74. Note that the simplifying assumption that all labor is unskilled has already been made here, so that we can forget the complication of the social reduction of skilled to unskilled labor.

24. It should, of course, be reiterated here that this socializing function of exchange presupposes only a limited amount of monopoly in the society; beyond a certain point of monopoly development, exchange would cease to play its initial social role.

25. Of course, as we will see, Volume I by no means ignores the competitive interaction of capitalists; but it deals with it only insofar as it effects the productive process, and as if this process were limited to many capitalists operating all in a single sphere.

26. Our choices here of *c* and *v* are not arbitrary. Marx calls capital invested in materials and machinery, which, one will recall, represents labor previously embodied in the production of these as commodities, "constant capital"; capital which purchases current labor, which unlike the former is not already embodied and thus is still exploitable in varying degrees, he calls "variable capital." We are ignoring here the further distinction between "stock" and "flow" capital as, for our purposes, it would only complicate matters to no good end.

27. Capital, III, 145–46.

28. Though here we have introduced this concept mainly for algebraic simplicity, it should be noted that as a measure of the intensity of labor exploitation it is a very central concept for Marx which will prove helpful in subsequent analyses involving the equations below.

29. *Capital,* III, 153.

30. Ibid., p. 195. Marx sees as a strength of his account that it not only explains the fact of a general profit rate but also why it is the particular rate that it is.

31. Ibid., p. 153. Cost-price is thus equal to $v + c'$ where c' equals, not the *total* constant capital advanced, but that share of it which is actually used up in production through consumption of raw materials and wear and tear on machinery. Profit, on the other hand, is calculated, as stated, on the full capital advanced as a share of all capital, that is, it is calculated on the percentage of the society's total capital which $c + v$ in its entirety represents.

32. The price of production of an item is thus equal to
$$(v + c') + p'(v + c')$$
where p' equals the average profit in the society.

33. This is the sense in which it is, as I have said at the beginning of the chapter, not fully analogous to the ideal gas laws of physics which never do.

34. *Capital*, III, 196–97.

35. See Marx's 1871 letter to Bolte, quoted in Chapter 3, in which he sets down in response to the latter's question his explicit views on the nature of politics.

36. See E. Böhm-Bawerk, *Karl Marx and the Close of his System* (London: Augustus Kelley, 1948). The original English edition was published in 1898, the German original in 1896, two years after the publication of vol. III of *Capital*.

37. Paul Sweezy, *The Theory of Capitalist Development* (New York: Monthly Review Press, 1970), pp. 109–15. The original edition was published in 1942. Bortkiewicz's paper was first published in 1907.

38. Marx's unfriendly critics are, of course, inclined to give him less credit than this, usually contenting themselves with the "disproof" of the labor theory and leaving matters there.

39. For an interesting critique of various "solutions" to the "transformation problem" see David Yaffe, "Value and Price in Marx's *Capital*," *Bulletin of the Conference of Socialist Economists* (Winter, 1974), 31–49, a work on which I rely very heavily in my discussion below as well.

40. They appear in Volumes I and II of *Capital* and are used only in connection with questions of the circulation of capital and to illustrate certain intrinsic features of a capitalistic economy which are more basic than those discussed above.

41. *Capital*, III, 164–65.

42. Prices of production are at best "the centre around which the daily market prices fluctuate" (*Capital*, III, 179); but even this view of them is, as Yaffe has noted, an idealization; merchant capital, banking capital, and rent all will modify market prices, as Marx subsequently points out. See Yaffe, p. 34; see also Kenneth May,

"Value and Price of Production: A Note on the Winternitz Solution," *The Economic Journal* (December, 1948), LVIII, pp. 596–99. If one is really interested in formulating a theory of prices, observes May, "the relationship between value and price of production is hardly more than a formal preliminary."

43. Yaffe, p. 46.

44. *Capital,* I, 592.

45. Ibid., p. 633.

46. Ibid., p. 613.

47. Ibid., p. 638.

48. This address, composed in English, was delivered in two parts on June 20 and 27, 1865; it was published only long after Marx's death by his daughter, Eleanor, under the title *Value, Price and Profit* (New York: International Publishers, 1935). The above quote is found in this edition on p. 61.

49. *Capital,* I, 645.

50. *Value, Price and Profit,* p. 61.

51. Even some sympathetic critics on the left have found this the Achilles' heel of Marxist theory and reconciled themselves to using Marxism as an ethical critique of capitalism's spiritual failure alone.

52. The reader is here referred to the account of dialectics given in Chapter 4.

53. Child labor laws, though usually viewed today as purely humanitarian measures, were, it should be remembered, pressed for by labor largely to protect the adult wage-scale which, as we have seen, the cheaper child labor undermined in a very serious way.

54. Such economic struggles, of course, tend always to broaden into the political realm anyway, so the situation here described could probably never obtain. In *Value, Price and Profit,* Marx is—we should not forget—arguing against the Owenite, John Weston, who even opposed *economic* actions, so his task is threefold—to defend labor actions, to defend their politicalization, and to argue for an ultimately revolutionary politics.

55. As we shall see in the next section, the stress caused by labor's victories, moreover, will—on Marx's view—intensify as time passes and capital expands.

56. *Capital,* III, 232–40.

57. The old methods, that is to say, since they no longer represent socially necessary labor-time, fail to add the value which they did formerly to their product, as new more efficient methods are introduced to produce it.

58. *Capital,* III, 250. Note how clearly the above conflict expresses the general dialectical form.

59. Ibid., p. 247.

60. Ibid., p. 239; italics mine.

61. Fisk, pp. 13–21. Data on the actual profit rate tend to be inconclusive as Fisk here shows. The construction of this entire section, it should be noted, owes much to the influence of this essay, which provides perhaps the clearest exposition of dialectics in Marx to appear in English to date.

62. Imperialism might, of course, also be involved in the cheapening of constant capital, so that colonial struggles also might be implicated in the determination at times. Fisk, however, tends to bring imperialist relations into the process somewhat marginally.

63. Fisk, p. 1.

64. Ibid., p. 16.

65. Ibid., p. 17. Although it is beyond the scope of my exposition here to examine them, I should add that Fisk in his essay does not content himself with merely pointing out the relevant phenomena; he also tries to show that Marx's analysis provides a *better* explanation for them than do several alternative approaches.

66. Ibid., p. 30. To see why the contradiction would tend to generate a shortage of capital, it need only be remembered that self-expansion of capital itself leads to a falling profit rate.

Chapter Seven

1. *Grundrisse,* trans. Martin Nicolaus (Harmondsworth: Penguin, 1973), pp. 704–9.

2. *Capital,* III, 820. For the entire passage from which this remark is taken, see the third chapter of this work.

3. *Grundrisse,* p. 708.

4. To see that P's tendency to fall as industry develops is an aspect of the contradiction, it is only necessary to note that, as less surplus per unit product is obtained, the more there is a temptation to use "disposable time" for production of surplus in an effort to keep surplus growing despite this fact.

5. Fisk (p. 17) notes that in manufacturing it has remained constant at 40.5 hours since 1947.

6. B. Kremen, "No Pride in this Dust," *Dissent,* (Winter, 1972), XIX, no. 86, 21–28. See also Peter Taylor, "The Sons of Bitches Just Won't Work: Postal Workers Against the State," *Zerowork*: *Political Materials 1* (December, 1975). This latter journal develops a slightly different version of the theme I present here; I am nonetheless indebted to its editorial collective and their associates for many of the thoughts I express above.

7. For an interesting perspective on this, see Guido Baldi, "Theses on Mass Worker and Social Capital," *Radical America* 6, no. 1 (May–June, 1972) pp. 3–21.

8. The countercultural attitude to the modern is, of course, not purely sentimental, being in part motivated by ecological considerations; but even here the approach to ecology tends to be utopian and marked by exemplary rather than political action.

9. In the only area where it has in any sense politicized to date—the mass movement against the war in Vietnam—it still carried with it many sentimental attitudes of an almost Luddite nature. For a good deal of the mystique that surrounded the National Liberation Front for the young derived from the fact that, seemingly with sheer will, they resisted the technologically sophisticated weaponry that the MacNamara's and Johnson's were certain would beat them.

10. Though this is not the place to argue such things at length, it is clear that the Russian Revolution was hardly in the long run a success, and that *in some measure at least* Lenin's policies must be held responsible for this. I assume, by the way, that a world socialist revolution would encompass the so-called Communist World as well as the capitalist nations per se.

Selected Bibliography

PRIMARY SOURCES

A complete edition of both Marx and Engels's works was published in East Berlin between 1958 and 1968 by the Institut für Marxismus-Leninismus. Entitled *Marx/Engels Werke*, it consists of thirty-nine volumes plus supplements. An English translation based on this edition is in the process of being published by International Publishers, New York, under the title, *Marx/Engels: Collected Works*. Begun in 1975, six volumes are available to date. The last covers the period 1845–1848.

Karl Marx: Early Writings. Translated and edited by T. B. Bottomore. New York: McGraw-Hill, 1963. This edition includes "On the Jewish Question," "Introduction: Critique of Hegel's Philosophy of Right," and the "Economic and Philosophical Manuscripts."

Early Writings: Marx. Translated by R. Livingstone and G. Benton. Baltimore: Penguin, 1975. This edition includes works not found in Bottomore's.

The German Ideology. Edited by R. Pascal. New York: International Publishers, 1947.

The Poverty of Philosophy. New York: International Publishers, 1963.

Grundrisse. Translated by Martin Nicolaus. Baltimore: Penguin, 1973.

Class Struggles in France. New York: International Publishers, 1964.

The 18th Brumaire of Louis Bonaparte. New York: International Publishers, 1963.

Pre-capitalist Economic Formations. Translated by E. J. Hobsbawm. New York: International Publishers, 1964. A selection from the "Grundrisse" notebooks.

A Contribution to the Critique of Political Economy. Translated by S. W. Ryazanskaya. Moscow: Progress Publishers, 1970.

Capital. 3 vols. Translated by S. Moore and E. Aveling. New York: International Publishers, 1967.

Theories of Surplus Value. Moscow: Progress Publishers, 1963.

Value, Price and Profit. New York: International Publishers, 1935.

Marx and Engels: Basic Writings on Politics & Philosophy. Edited by Lewis Feuer. Garden City, N. Y.: Doubleday, 1959.

189

Marx on Economics. Edited by Robert Freedman. New York: Harcourt, Brace & World, 1961. Selections with a running commentary.

Karl Marx: Political Writings. 3 vols. Edited by David Fernbach. New York: Random House, 1974.

SECONDARY SOURCES

ALTHUSSER, LOUIS. *For Marx.* New York: Random House, 1970. This book is heavily influenced by the official Communist Party line, but still interesting and scholarly.

AVINIERI, SHLOMO. *The Social and Political Thought of Karl Marx.* London: Cambridge University Press, 1968. Avinieri tends to lay far too great an emphasis on Marx's very early (pre 1844 *Manuscripts*) work, but his analysis is often helpful and insightful.

BÖHM-BAWERK, EUGEN VON. *Karl Marx and the Close of His System.* New York: Augustus Kelley, 1949. The classical economic critique of Marx.

ENGELS, FREDERICK. *Socialism: Utopian and Scientific.* New York: International Publishers, 1935. Engels's short 1878 account of Marxist theory.

FISK, MILTON. "Rate of Profit and Class Struggle." *Radical Philosophers' Newsjournal,* no. 5 (August, 1975) pp. 1–37. A brilliant article which includes a fine account of the nature of Marx's dialectic.

HOOK, SIDNEY. *From Hegel to Marx.* 1936. Ann Arbor: University of Michigan Press, 1962. A good account of Marx's early influences together with some interesting work on dialectics.

KORSCH, KARL. *Karl Marx.* London: Chapman and Hall, 1938. A fine introduction to Marxist theory.

LEFEBVRE, HENRI. *Dialectical Materialism.* London: Jonathan Cape, 1968. A somewhat confusing but at times helpful account of Marx's methodology.

LENIN, V. I. *The Teachings of Karl Marx.* New York: International Publishers, 1964. Lenin's short introduction to Marx's theory is good for its purposes, but limited in its scope.

MARCUSE, HERBERT. *Reason and Revolution.* 1941. Boston: Beacon, 1960. Professor Marcuse insists on leaving Marx an Hegelian his entire life; but the book is of value for its understanding of Hegel's views on politics, and their subsequent influence on Marx.

MATTICK, PAUL. *Marx and Keynes.* London: Sargent, 1969. A

dense but fascinating work on modern Keynsian policy in the light of Marxist theory.

McLELLAN, DAVID. *Karl Marx: His Life and Thought.* New York: Harper & Row, 1974. One of the most recent contributions to Marxology by a good scholar.

MEHRING, FRANZ. *Karl Marx.* Ann Arbor: University of Michigan Press, 1962. Mehring is the most famous of Marx's biographers.

OLLMAN, BERTELL. *Alienation: Marx's Conception of Man in Capitalist Society.* London: Cambridge University Press, 1971. An overly philosophical account of Marx.

RIAZANOV, DAVID. *Karl Marx and Friedrich Engels.* New York: Monthly Review Press, 1973. Despite Riazanov's insistence that Marx and Engels were veritable saints, this is a useful and thorough biography.

RUBIN, I. *Essays on Marx's Theory of Value.* 1928. Detroit: Black and Red, 1972. An excellent account of Marxist economic theory.

SWEEZY, PAUL. *The Theory of Capitalist Development.* New York: Monthly Review Press, 1942. Despite its errors, Sweezy's text is a good introduction to Marxist economic theory, both well written and uncomplicated.

WILSON, EDMUND. *To the Finland Station.* Garden City, N. Y.: Doubleday, 1940. Edmund Wilson does not understand Marxism very well, but he writes beautifully and brings Marx's biography to life in a way that no one else can. The book is also valuable as a source of background information.

YAFFE, DAVID. "Value and Price in Marx's Capital." *Bulletin of the Conference of Socialist Economists* (Winter, 1974) pp. 31–49. Yaffe's essay dispels the confusions of the "transformation problem" very clearly; an excellent work on Marx's economic theory.

Index

Absolute Idealism, 80

Abstract labor, 124-25, 132-33

Accumulation, 59, *142-46*

Agriculture, 38; Asiatic mode of production and, 36; rise of capitalism and, 49; transition to communism and, 62, 63

Alienation, 87, *104-20*

Althusser, Louis, 70, 104, 118, 119

Anarchism, 24

Ancient mode of production, 31, *33-37*, 42

Anti-Duhring (Engels), 100

Aristotle, 81

Artisans, 16; rise of capitalism and, 166n35; rise of medieval city and, 40

Asiatic (Oriental) mode of production, 31, *32-33*, 36, 37, 42

Avinieri, Shlomo, 63, 65

Babeuf, Gracchus, 16

Bakunin, Michael, 16, *25-27*

Barbarians, 37, 38

Bauer, Bruno, 12, 13, 17

Bell, Daniel, 104

Berlin University, 12

Bismark, 162n15

Blanqui, Auguste, 24

Blanquists, 70, 71, 72

Blue collar workers, 157-58

Böhm-Bawerk, Eugene, 138

Bolte, Friedrich, 74

Bonn University, 12, 13

Bookchin, Murray, 75-76

Bortkiewicz, Ladislaus von, 138, 139

Bourgeois mode of production, 31, *42-54*; *see also* Capitalism

Bourgeoisie (Capitalist class; ruling

192

class): class struggle and, 28-30; and dialectics of capitalism, 96; dictatorship of the, 71-72; force and, 73-76; ideological viewpoint of, *128-30*, 131; Marxian science and, 101; Paris Commune and, 26

Brandt, Willy, 73

British Museum, 21

Capital (Marx): 22, 51, 58, 97, 98, 101, 103, 105, 114, 117, 119, 120, 128-29, 145; Volumn I ("The Process of Capitalist Production"), 22, 31, 63, 102, 110, 116, 121, 122, 133, 136, 144, 154; Volumn II ("The Process of Circulation of Capital"), 27, 121; Volumn III ("The Process of Capitalist Production as a Whole"), 27, 31, 59-60, 68, 121, 130-31, 133, 136-38; Volumn IV ("Theories of Surplus Value"), 22, 121

Capital, 110; accumulation of, 59, *142-46*; and development of capitalism, 43, 45; falling rate of profit and, 147-53; organic composition of, *134-36*, 138, 148; as power over surplus, 130-31; surplus value and, 134-37

Capitalism: accumulation process of, 142-46; bourgeois mode of production and, 31, *42-54*; contradictions of contemporary, 154-59; dialectic relation of wage worker and capitalist in, 96-97; economic structure of, 122-33; falling rate of profit and, 147-53; Marx's theory of alienation and, 104-20; and transition to